McGraw-Hill's

CAREERS FOR

AQUATIC
TYPES

& Others Who Want to Make a Splash

Careers for You Series

McGraw-Hill's

CAREERS FOR

AQUATIC TYPES

& Others Who Want to Make a Splash

BLYTHE CAMENSON

SECOND EDITION

New York Chicago San Francisco Lisbon London Madrid Mexico City
Milan New Delhi San Juan Seoul Singapore Sydney Toronto

The *McGraw·Hill* Companies

Library of Congress Cataloging-in-Publication Data

Camenson, Blythe.
    Careers for aquatic types & others who want to make a splash / by Blythe
Camenson — 2nd ed.
        p. cm. — (McGraw-Hill careers for you series)
        ISBN 0-07-148215-6 (alk. paper)
        1. Aquatic sciences—Vocational guidance. I. Title.

GC30.5.C36 2008
333.702—dc22   2007010786

1 2 3 4 5 6 7 8 9 10 11 12 13 14 15 DOC/DOC 1 0 9 8 7

ISBN 978-0-07-148215-8
MHID   0-07-148215-6

McGraw-Hill books are available at special quantity discounts to use as premiums and
sales promotions, or for use in corporate training programs. For more information,
please write to the Director of Special Sales, Professional Publishing, McGraw-Hill,
Two Penn Plaza, New York, NY 10121-2298. Or contact your local bookstore.

This book is printed on acid-free paper.

Contents

Acknowledgments

The author would like to thank Brad Crawford for his assistance in preparing this edition.

Introduction: Getting Your Feet Wet

There's something about spending time near, on, or in the water. Just as our undersea friends, whether mammals, fish, or plants, find the shallowest areas of oceans and seas to be the most hospitable, we gravitate to shorelines that teem with life. Water brings with it lush flora, temperature-moderating breezes, recreational opportunities, a ready form of transportation, and an entirely new dimension to explore. Coastal communities are popular, then, but most major cities have some strategic waterfront location, whether along a riverbank or lakeshore, so inland cities are by no means left high and dry.

As you might expect of a resource with such diverse assets, the careers tied to it are equally diverse. Responsibilities, day-to-day experiences, compensation, and educational requirements are all over the map. You could work as a dive instructor, ship or ferry captain, marine scientist, cruise director, navy officer, or a fisherman. Let's dive into what sorts of jobs are available and see what they entail.

Aquatic Careers

We'll cover a variety of job options, but this list is by no means exhaustive. As you do your own research and investigate how you might combine your love of the water with a satisfying career, you will no doubt think of others.

- *Aquatic science* is the general term for research conducted in oceans and coastal or inland waters connected to the sea. Under this broad category fall oceanographers, marine mammalogists, geologists, and archaeologists, to name a few. See Chapter 1.
- The navy and coast guard, whether American or Canadian, offer good opportunities for hearty young seafarers. From patrolling inland waters for the coast guard to working as a journalist for the navy, you can find a place to put your skills to good use. See Chapter 2.
- Commercial fishing involves hard work, long hours, and seasonal fluctuations, but those who love independence and open water are drawn to it. The proportion of self-employed workers in fishing is among the highest of any field. See Chapter 3.
- Water transportation workers operate and maintain all sorts of seagoing vessels, including tugboats, cargo ships, and ferries. The career options, from captain to crew to engineer, are broad and plentiful. See Chapter 4.
- Every day's a vacation day when you're part of a cruise staff. The work can be fun and exciting, with the opportunity to travel to exotic ports and meet different kinds of people. Jobs run the gamut from kitchen help to purser to activities director. See Chapter 5.
- Water safety offers a wide range of employment opportunities, from lifeguarding at summer camps to rescue duties with the National Park Service. See Chapter 6.
- Jobs in water recreation allow you to pass on your skills to others while you enjoy the sun and surf. Adult education programs, summer camps, the Red Cross, YMCAs, private resorts, and many other organizations employ instructors to teach swimming, sailing, and related aquatic activities. See Chapter 7.

Questions to Ask Yourself

People who work in and around the water give of themselves in many different capacities, providing valuable services—and having fun. Perhaps you aren't sure of the working conditions in different fields or which areas would best suit your personality, skills, and lifestyle.

There are several factors to consider when deciding which sector to pursue. Each field carries with it different levels of responsibility and commitment.

To narrow your occupational choices, you need to know what each job involves. Ask yourself the following questions and make note of your answers. Then, as you read through the following seven chapters, compare your needs and expectations with the overviews of specific career options.

- How much time are you willing to commit to training? Some skills can be learned on the job or in a year or two of formal training; others take considerably longer.
- Do you want to work on land or at sea? Should your job free you of all desk and office-related accoutrements?
- Can you handle a certain amount of stress on the job, or would you prefer a low-key environment?
- How much money do you expect to earn?
- Do you want to be your own boss, or would you be content as a salaried employee?
- Would you rather work during the day, or are evenings or weekends acceptable? Can you handle being away from home for long stretches of time?

In many of the chapters, you will also read firsthand accounts from people working in the field. Their comments could help you pinpoint the careers that would interest you. What better way to learn about a career than from someone who's already established and experienced?

Knowing what your expectations are and comparing them to the realities of the work will help you make informed choices.

Additional Resources

No single publication can tell you everything you need to know about a given job or field. In the Appendix and throughout the book, you'll find references to helpful websites and contact information for relevant professional organizations. To make the most of your career search, consider using all of these tools in combination. Now, full speed ahead to all those job possibilities!

McGraw-Hill's

CAREERS FOR

AQUATIC TYPES

& Others Who Want to Make a Splash

CHAPTER ONE

Underwater Science

A career in the aquatic sciences could take you to the ends of the earth or a stone's throw from your hometown. The distance is up to you. Many aspiring aquatic and marine biologists decide to pursue the field because of an affinity for marine mammals, the effortlessly charming dolphins, whales, manatees, seals, and otters that make a science career seem so idyllic. But aquatic science offers much more than just working with marine mammals. Sometimes considered a subfield of botany or zoology, aquatic science encompasses several fields and career paths—in fact, many universities offer separate programs or departments in its various aspects.

Breakdown of the Aquatic Sciences

Aquatic scientists study virtually everything having to do with water. For example, aquatic chemists research organic, inorganic, and trace-metal chemistry. Marine geologists study how ocean basins were formed and how geothermal and other geological processes interact with seawater. Freshwater geologists may study past climates or the organisms found in sediments. Aquatic scientists could also study processes that last for a second or for a million years. They might study one small estuary or an entire ocean.

Aquatic science is interdisciplinary. While most aquatic scientists specialize in just one area, they use information from all fields and often work together with related scientists in teams. For example, chemists and biologists might work together to understand the ways in which the chemical components of bodies of water interact with plants, animals, and microorganisms such as bacteria.

Oceanography

Oceanography is the study of the biological, chemical, geological, optical, and physical characteristics of oceans and estuaries. Its subfields include physical oceanography, chemical oceanography, biological oceanography, and geological and geophysical oceanography.

- **Physical oceanographers** study currents, waves, and motion and the interaction of light, radar, heat, sound, and wind with the sea. They are also interested in the interaction between the ocean and atmosphere and the relationship of the sea, weather, and climate.
- **Chemical oceanographers** study chemical compounds and the many chemical interactions that occur in the ocean and on the ocean floor.
- **Biological oceanographers** are interested in describing the diverse life forms in the sea, their population densities, and their natural environments. They try to understand how these animals and plants exist in interrelationships with other sea life and also focus on the impact of human intervention on the oceanic environment.
- **Geological and geophysical oceanographers** study the shape, nature, and origin of the material of the seafloor.

Oceanographers also usually include ocean scientists, ocean engineers, and ocean technicians.

- **Ocean scientists** investigate how the oceans work. They usually have graduate degrees in oceanography with bachelor's degrees in one of the fundamental science fields such as biology, physics, chemistry, or geology.

- **Ocean engineers** perform the usual tasks of any engineers—such as designing a structure—but they deal with specific issues related to that structure and its environment in the sea. An ocean engineer might design supports for oil well drilling equipment that stands on the ocean floor. They must take into account all information about ocean currents and the force they exert on the structure, plus saltwater corrosion, marine-life interference, and other similar elements. Ocean engineers also design the equipment oceanographers use to make oceanographic measurements.

- **Ocean technicians** are responsible for equipment calibration and preparation, measurements and sampling at sea, instrument maintenance and repair, and data processing. Ocean technicians usually have bachelor's degrees, although some may be successful at finding work with two-year associate's degrees.

Marine Biology

Marine biology refers specifically to saltwater environments and covers a surprisingly wide variety of disciplines. Examples include planetology, meteorology, physics, chemistry, geology, physical oceanography, paleontology, and biology. Marine science also includes archaeology, anthropology, sociology, engineering, and other studies of human relationships with the sea.

Limnology

Limnology involves the same concerns as oceanography but is limited to inland systems such as lakes, rivers, streams, ponds, and wetlands and includes both freshwater and saltwater systems. Physical limnologists study water movements while optical limnologists study the transmission of light through the water.

Marine Mammalogy

Marine mammalogists study ocean-dwelling mammals in three orders: the pinnipeds, flipper-limbed carnivores such as sea lions and walruses; cetaceans, which include whales and dolphins; and sirenians, such as manatees. Marine mammal scientists work to understand these animals' genetic, systematic, and evolutionary relationships; population structures; community dynamics; anatomy and physiology; behavior and sensory abilities; parasites and diseases; and geographic and microhabitat distributions. Marine mammal scientists also study ecology, management, and conservation. You could be a field biologist, fishery vessel observer, animal-care specialist, trainer, whale-watch guide, or conservationist.

Archaeology

Archaeology is a subfield of anthropology. Archaeologists study the artifacts of past cultures to learn about history, customs, and living habits. They study the research of other archaeologists and survey and excavate archaeological sites, recording and cataloging their finds. By careful analysis, archaeologists reconstruct earlier cultures and determine their influences on the present.

Most people imagine excavation on land when they think of archaeology, but there are two subfields of particular interest to aquatic types: Nautical archaeology is the study of shipwreck sites, either on land or underwater. Underwater archaeology is the study and excavation of submerged sites. Usually these are shipwrecks, but underwater archaeology includes the study of submerged habitation sites as well, such as villages flooded by construction of a dam.

Who Hires Aquatic Scientists?

Aquatic scientists find jobs with colleges and universities, international organizations, federal and state agencies, private companies, nonprofit laboratories, local governments, aquariums, zoos, marine parks, and museums. They also might be self-employed. Some of the government agencies that hire aquatic scientists:

UNITED STATES
Army Corps of Engineers
Department of Agriculture
Department of Commerce
Department of Defense
Department of Energy
Department of the Interior
Department of State
Environmental Protection Agency
Marine Mammal Commission
Minerals Management Service
National Aeronautics and Space Administration
National Marine Fisheries Service
National Oceanic and Atmospheric Administration
National Park Service
National Science Foundation
Natural Resources Conservation Service
U.S. Fish and Wildlife Service
U.S. National Biological Service

CANADA
Canadian Environmental Assessment Agency
Environment Canada
Fisheries and Oceans Canada
National Defence
Natural Resources Canada
Parks Canada

But federal governments aren't the only places aquatic scientists find employment. Private industries, such as commercial fishing and oil and gas exploration, production, and transportation, hire aquatic scientists when their operations affect marine mammals or raise environmental concerns. Many legal firms and environmental, advocacy, and animal-welfare organizations also depend on aquatic scientists and use them for legal or policy development, problem solving, and regulatory and administrative roles.

Aquariums, marine parks, and zoos hire specialists for veterinary care, husbandry, training, research, and education programs. Examples of marine mammal jobs include researcher, field biologist, fishery vessel observer, laboratory technician, animal trainer, animal-care specialist, veterinarian, whale-watch guide, naturalist, and educator. Museums hire specialists for educational programs, research, and curatorial positions. Magazines, book publishers, and television and radio stations also provide employment for specialists, but usually on a part-time freelance or consulting basis.

Later in this chapter, you will find a close-up look at aquarium work, along with firsthand accounts from professionals employed in aquariums in different capacities.

What to Expect

Many aquatic science researchers spend time each year engaged in fieldwork, collecting data and samples in natural environments. The data are collected during research cruises on small or large vessels, and the amount of time at sea can last from one week to more than two months and involve a team of scientists from many disciplines.

Limnological data most often are collected during short, one- to two-day field trips that are usually narrow in scope. At the other extreme, trips can involve stays at field stations lasting from days to months.

When not in the field, aquatic research scientists spend most of their time in the laboratory running experiments or at the computer analyzing data or developing models. They also study papers in scientific journals, relate that research to their own work, and write papers for publication.

Those working at universities must couple lectures and student conferences with their own research. In any environment, attending meetings is also part of the job. Scientists may also spend time writing research proposals to obtain grant money for more research.

For aquatic scientists with administrative jobs, the time is spent in the office or communicating with colleagues and the public. Like any research scientists, they also attend national or international conferences to keep up in their fields. Hands-on workers, such as those involved with marine mammals or working in aquariums, have jobs that are not as glamorous as movies or TV programs depict. The work involves hard labor, such as lugging buckets of fish and cleaning tanks in addition to time spent interacting with the animals.

How to Get Started

Most entry-level jobs require a bachelor's degree in a natural science from an accredited institution. (A few entry-level positions take high school graduates, but the opportunities for career advancement are limited.) Because most bachelor's degree programs do not require research experience, applicants may expect to participate as research assistants and advance mostly on the basis of on-the-job experience.

Many companies look for a master's degree from applicants, especially where research is part of the job description. A doctorate is usually necessary for academic positions or in other settings where the employee would manage other scientists and conduct his or her own studies.

Job opportunities are varied and exist at all educational levels, but as with other fields, the higher-level and better-paying jobs require the most education. Because aquatic science encompasses so many specializations, undergraduate biology students benefit from the broadest education possible. There is no guarantee you'll get a job in your area of interest or specialization—at least not right away. Because of this, a general education provides a foundation for entering many types of employment. Before specializing, aquatic scientists usually have a background in one or more of the basic sciences, such as biology, chemistry, geology, mathematics, or physics.

Many of the disciplines in aquatic science, such as marine biology, are graduate-level pursuits, so when choosing your undergraduate program, it's a good idea to investigate the strengths and specializations of the biology programs. If you know you want to pursue graduate work in marine science, for example, then earning your undergraduate degree at a university that offers courses in that area will help when applying to graduate schools. But graduate schools prefer students to major in a core science, such as biology, physics, chemistry, or geology, rather than a specialized subject such as limnology or oceanography.

You can specialize in the areas that interest you the most, but not at the expense of related course work. You should still be sure to add statistics, mathematics, computers, and data management to your curriculum. Good oral and written communication skills are crucial, as they are in any profession. And many careers in marine mammal science require additional qualifications such as scuba certification and boat-handling experience.

To enhance your employability, consider contributing to a research project in a science laboratory. You could do this as a supervised independent study, working with a particular professor's research project, or through an internship, work-study job, or a stint of volunteering. If your university doesn't offer any of these opportunities, seek out other aquatic scientists, perhaps working at a local aquarium or marine science center, and volunteer to help in any way you can.

In addition, many summer research programs are available at universities with graduate-level limnology or oceanography programs. These summer research experiences are usually offered to students after they have completed their sophomore or junior years and offer a good chance to learn more about the discipline as a possible career choice. You can find out about these programs by consulting colleges that offer graduate degrees in limnology or oceanography. (See the American Society of Limnology and Oceanography's list of programs worldwide at www.aslo.org/education/links/academic.html.) The programs are open to students from all universities.

To further prepare yourself, you can also attend seminars and join aquatic science organizations, such as the American Society of Limnology and Oceanography mentioned above. By doing so, you will better understand the field and start making contacts in the community of people in which you'll eventually work. Get involved in projects, talk to scientists, and participate in any way you can.

Aquatic Science Programs

You can find information on colleges and universities offering programs in aquatic science and all its subfields online (search by college or major at search engines such as www.collegetoolkit.com or www.gradschools.com) and through such directories as Peterson's (www.petersons.com), which is available at school guidance centers, public libraries, and online. You will find the programs listed under various headings:

Aquatic Science
Biology
Chemistry
Earth Science
Geology
Limnology
Marine Biology
Marine Ecology
Meteorology
Ocean Engineering
Oceanography
Physics

Career Outlook

In general, opportunities are good for those with a bachelor's degree or higher in science. But some specialty areas present stiff competition to job applicants. Those with a doctorate (Ph.D.) who want to conduct research face strong competition for tenured positions at universities, for example, and marine mammalogy inevitably attracts many more candidates than the market can accommodate.

Opportunities for those with a bachelor's or master's degree in biological science should be better. The number of science-related jobs for which those without Ph.D.s usually qualify is expected to exceed the number of independent research positions. Non-Ph.D.s also may fill positions as science or engineering technicians or as medical health technologists or technicians. Some may become high school biology teachers.

Advances in biotechnology over the past two decades rapidly expanded the market for biological scientists, but that has slowed down somewhat since. However, much of the basic biological research done in recent years has resulted in new knowledge, and companies will find new commercial uses for it in the coming years—even those that don't engage strictly in biotechnology work.

In addition, efforts to discover new ways to clean up and preserve the environment will continue to add to job growth. More biological scientists will be needed to determine the environmental impact of industry and government actions and to prevent or correct environmental problems such as the negative effects of pesticide use. Some aquatic scientists will find opportunities in environmental regulatory agencies; others will use their expertise to advise lawmakers on legislation to save environmentally sensitive areas.

There will continue to be demand in botany, zoology, and marine biology, but opportunities will be limited because of the small size of these fields. Prospective marine biology students should be aware that those who would like to enter this specialty far outnumber the few openings available each year for the types of glamorous research jobs many would like to have. Almost all marine biologists who do basic research have a Ph.D.

It is important to remember that job opportunities and openings in all fields can change quickly, however. Even when the number of available positions in this career path is small, top scientists are always in demand. If you follow your interests, work hard, make contacts, and don't give up, you'll get your shot.

. . . .

Earnings

Aquatic scientists enter this field for the love of their work—not for the money. The salary you'll earn will depend in part on your educational background, experience, responsibilities, area of specialization, number of years of service, and the size, type, and geographical location of the employing institution. In general, jobs in private industry have the highest pay, followed by jobs with the government.

Biologists with bachelor's degrees in one of the life sciences started at an average of $31,000 in 2005. The median salary for biological scientists in 2004 was $50,000. In 2005 biological scientists working for the U.S. government earned a median annual salary of $70,000. As senior scientists or full professors, doctorate degree holders with fifteen years of experience or more could earn in excess of $100,000 per year.

Salaries for aquarists and animal trainers vary depending upon the institution's funding and the size of its budget but tend to be lower than in the sciences overall. An entry-level aquarist could start at $25,000, and a midlevel aquarist might earn $35,000 a year. Salaries for senior and supervising aquarists vary the most and range from $45,000 to $120,000 for the most experienced scientists working at elite facilities.

Who's Who at the Aquarium

The collections in large public aquariums require a variety of specialists to maintain them: engineers, accountants, animal trainers, curators, aquarists, and biologists. Other departments within aquariums are conservation, veterinary services, design, research, education, marketing, and public relations. What follows is a sampling of typical science-related jobs found in aquariums.

Aquarists

Aquarists are the frontline people who take care of the exhibits. One of the primary skills an aquarist must bring to the job is nationally recognized certification as a scuba diver. (See "Becoming a Certified Diver" in this chapter and Chapter 7 for more information on diving credentials.) In addition to maintaining and cleaning the exhibits, aquarists are the primary people responsible for stocking them. Depending on the exhibit size, an aquarist will do a lot of diving, both inside the exhibit tanks and collecting from local waters.

There are several aquarist rankings, and the job titles vary depending upon the particular institution. In general they are aquarist-in-training, trained aquarist, senior aquarist, and supervisor. At the New England Aquarium (profiled later in this chapter), aquarists are also divided into two main categories: diving aquarists and gallery aquarists.

Diving aquarists dive into the large tank exhibit to maintain the health of the fish and to take care of the exhibit in general. Gallery aquarists are in charge of smaller exhibits but many more of them. Gallery aquarists also spend time in the water, but they aren't in a wet suit every day. Every aquarist gets wet, but some get wet more often than others.

All aquarists go on collecting trips and use their diving skills in that capacity, too. In addition, aquarists need fishing and boat-handling skills. At some institutions, as aquarists become more experienced, they are given opportunities to develop their own special niches, getting involved in research or conservation projects as well as participating in collecting trips.

Curators

An aquarium's general curator takes care of all husbandry matters. Under this top position's jurisdiction fall curators responsible for different areas of an aquarium's operation. For example, an aquarium could have curators of fishes, marine mammals, exhibit design, research, and conservation. These curator positions often involve more administrative than hands-on duties.

Trainers

At some institutions, trainers follow rankings similar to aquarists: assistant trainer (or trainer-in-training), trainer, senior trainer, and supervisor. Trainers are responsible for the care of animals and the exhibits as well as teaching presentation behaviors, research behaviors, and behaviors that allow for medical examination. For more information, see the trainer's firsthand account later in this chapter.

Becoming a Certified Diver

There are four or five nationally and internationally recognized certifying agencies. Future aquarists are responsible for obtaining this training and should do so in most instances before applying for an aquarist's position. Many university physical education departments offer diver training. It can also be pursued privately, through the YMCA, or through local dive shops, where full services are offered, including equipment use as well as training. See Chapter 7 for more information.

The Job Search

The community of marine professionals is close enough that finding out about openings is relatively easy. Someone always knows something. One good source for job announcements is the personnel departments of specific government agencies, private companies, and educational institutions, as well as museums, zoos, marine parks, and aquariums. Numerous resources can also keep you abreast of openings. Some are listed below; please see the Appendix for other resources.

Websites

American Fisheries Society
www.fisheries.org

American Society of Limnology and Oceanography
www.aslo.org/employment.html

Aquaculture Network Information Center
www.aquanic.org/text/job_serv.htm

Association of Zoos & Aquariums
www.aza.org/JobListings

Biology Jobs.Com
www.biologyjobs.com

EcoEmploy.com
www.ecoemploy.com

Marine Technology Society
www.mtsociety.org/employment

The Oceanography Society
www.tos.org/resources/job_annc.html

Public Service Commission of Canada (Canadian federal
   government jobs)
www.jobs-emplois.gc.ca

ScienceCareers.org
http://sciencecareers.sciencemag.org

ScienceJobs.com (*New Scientist Magazine*)
www.sciencejobs.com

USA Jobs (U.S. federal government jobs)
www.usajobs.gov

Networking

Although what you know is very important, who you know can sometimes give you the chance to prove it. Word-of-mouth and personal recommendations are the best and most reliable ways to secure jobs. Volunteers or interns are well placed to get a full-time job with their organizations because of their preliminary experience and relationship with the staff. A professor might recommend a graduate student he or she is supervising to a colleague. An informal interview at a scientific conference you attend could result in a job offer.

Networking is less daunting than it might seem. Everyone needs help, and everyone knows people that their colleagues don't know. Sharing information, strategies, contacts, and experiences is a great way to improve yourself professionally as well as meet people you're in a position to help—and those who might be able to help you. Don't confine your professional interactions to people who work in the same field. If you're conducting a job search, for example, let your family, friends, and the guy who does your dry cleaning know what kind of job you're interested in and allow social power to spread the word.

Internships

Internships are an excellent way to get your foot in the door. When full-time openings come up, employers would rather hire someone they know and have worked with. Employers can also provide interns with referrals to job opportunities and recommendations to go along with future job applications. Though often competitive, internships need not be scary to apply for. Established professionals are frequently thrilled to share their acquired knowledge with an enthusiastic newcomer, and serving in a good internship is a win-win. If you perform well and enjoy the work, you have a great advantage when it comes time to enter the job market. And if you discover that the work isn't for you, you've saved yourself many years of heartache in pursuing a career you didn't really want.

The most important factor is the intern experience. Whether paid or unpaid—and unfortunately, many are unpaid—look for internships that put you in regular contact with professionals at the peak of their profession, that allow you to learn firsthand and take on substantive duties, and that are part of a formal program where someone is responsible for overseeing and reviewing your work and conveying your achievements to others, in the form of college credit or letters of recommendation to future employers. Don't forget to ask about fringe benefits or incidentals: free or reduced-rate meals or housing, roommate-matching services, paid travel from your city, and whether any associated equipment will be provided or must be purchased.

Following is a lengthy, but not exhaustive, list of internships available regularly to people training in aquatic science. Visit the websites for more information about length and seasonality, pay, prerequisites, competitiveness, and other details.

American Cetacean Society
PO Box 1391
San Pedro, CA 90733
www.acsonline.org

Aquarium of Niagara Falls
Intern/Volunteer Program
701 Whirlpool Street
Niagara Falls, NY 14301
www.aquariumofniagara.org

Brookfield Zoo
Internship Program
3300 Golf Road
Brookfield, IL 60513
www.brookfieldzoo.org

Cetacean Behavior Laboratory
San Diego State University
1624 Veteran Avenue, #3
Los Angeles, CA 90024
www.sci.sdsu.edu/CBL/CBLHome.html

Clearwater Marine Aquarium
249 Windward Passage
Clearwater, FL 33767
www.cmaquarium.org

Dolphin Dreams Images
PMB 529, Suite B-1A
74-5533 Luhia Street
Kailua-Kona, HI 96740
www.dolphindreams.com

The Dolphin Institute
PO Box 700694
Kapolei, HI 96709
www.dolphin-institute.org

Dolphins Plus
31 Corrine Place
Key Largo, FL 33037
www.dolphinsplus.com

Earthwatch Institute
3 Clock Tower Place, Suite 100
Box 75
Maynard, MA 01754
www.earthwatch.org

Fish and Wildlife Research Institute
(Florida Fish and Wildlife Conservation Commission)
100 Eighth Avenue SE
St. Petersburg, FL 33701
www.research.myfwc.com

Long Marine Lab
Pinniped Research in Cognition & Sensory Systems
University of California–Santa Cruz
100 Shaffer Road
Santa Cruz, CA 95060
http://pinnipedlab.ucsc.edu

Mote Marine Laboratory
1600 Ken Thompson Parkway
Sarasota, FL 34236
www.mote.org

Mystic Aquarium & Institute for Exploration
55 Coogan Boulevard
Mystic, CT 06355
www.mysticaquarium.org

National Aquarium in Baltimore
Pier 3
501 East Pratt Street
Baltimore, MD 21202
www.aqua.org

National Museum of Natural History
Academic Resources Center
PO Box 37012
NHB, MRC 106, Room 59A
Washington, DC 20013
www.nmnh.si.edu/rtp/other_opps/internship_summary.html

National Zoo (Smithsonian National Zoological Park)
3001 Connecticut Avenue NW
Washington, DC 20008
www.nationalzoo.si.edu

Newfound Harbor Marine Institute
1300 Big Pine Avenue
Big Pine Key, FL 33043
www.nhmi.org

New England Aquarium
Intern/Volunteer Program
Central Wharf
Boston, MA 02110
www.neaq.org

New York Aquarium
The Wildlife Conservation Society
2300 Southern Boulevard
Bronx, NY 10460
www.nyaquarium.com

The Ocean Conservancy
2029 K Street, NW
Washington, DC 20006
www.oceanconservancy.org

The Oceania Project
PO Box 646
Byron Bay, NSW 2481
Australia
www.oceania.org.au

Pacific Whale Foundation
300 Maalaea Road, Suite 211
Wailuku, HI 96793
www.pacificwhale.org

Provincetown Center for Coastal Studies
115 Bradford Street
Provincetown, MA 02657
www.coastalstudies.org

School for Field Studies
10 Federal Street, Suite 24
Salem, MA 01970
www.fieldstudies.org

John G. Shedd Aquarium
1200 South Lake Shore Drive
Chicago, IL 60605
www.sheddaquarium.org

Tethys Research Institute
Viale G.B. Gadio 2
20121 Milano
Italy
www.tethys.org

Theater of the Sea
84721 Overseas Highway
Islamorada, FL 33036
www.theaterofthesea.com

Waikiki Aquarium
University of Hawaii–Manoa
2777 Kalakaua Avenue
Honolulu, HI 96815
www.waquarium.org

Whale Center of New England
Intern/Volunteer Program
24 Harbor Loop
PO Box 159
Gloucester, MA 01931
www.whalecenter.org

Whale Museum
62 First Street North
PO Box 945
Friday Harbor, WA 98250
www.whale-museum.org

Whale Research Group
Department of Industry, Trade and Technology
Memorial University of Newfoundland
PO Box 8700
St. John's, NL A1B 4J6
Canada
www.compusult.nf.ca/ditt/wrg.htm

Field Programs

While some internships provide interns with a stipend as well as college credit, other programs charge fees to participate. Known as field programs, these are not meant to reproduce the experience of working on staff, but rather to orient a select group to the basics of marine science and maximize contact with animals and time in the field. Like internships, field programs can yield valuable insights into career paths and increase your visibility when a door opens at the right time. In addition to the programs listed below, you can refer to Green Volunteers' *World Guide* and Information Network to Voluntary Work in Nature Conservation, a print guide with online supplements, for numerous volunteer opportunities that could give you a similar experience. (See also the resources online at www.greenvolunteers.com.)

Coastal Ecosystems Research Foundation
Allison Harbour
PO Box 122
Port Hardy, BC V0N 2P0
Canada
www.cerf.bc.ca

Mingan Island Cetacean Study
285 Green Street
St. Lambert, QC J4P 1T3
Canada
http://whale.wheelock.edu/whalenet-stuff/mics.html

Oceanic Society
Fort Mason QRTS 35
San Francisco, CA 94123
www.oceanic-society.org

School for Field Studies
10 Federal Street
Salem, MA 01970
www.fieldstudies.org

What It's Really Like

The people in the following three profiles work in various positions at the New England Aquarium in Boston, Massachusetts. The New England Aquarium is one of the premiere showcases for the display of marine life and habitats. Its mission is to "increase understanding of aquatic life and environments, to enable people to act to conserve the world of water, and to provide leadership for the preservation and sustainable use of aquatic resources." The aquarium pursues these goals through exhibits, education, conservation, and research programs. Exhibits showcase the diversity, importance, and beauty of aquatic life and habitats and highlight aquatic conservation issues of importance.

The major centerpiece for the aquarium is the two-hundred-thousand-gallon Caribbean Coral Reef Exhibit, which rises through four stories of the facility. Visitors are afforded a multi-angle view of sea turtles, sharks, moray eels, and the other tropical fish that live inside. The facility takes a special interest in conservation and monitoring of critical marine habitats, and one section of the aquarium, the Aquarium Medical Center, offers visitors a glimpse into the staff's work of rescuing, diagnosing, and treating sick and injured wild animals. Examination-room cameras send images to remote monitors in real time, allowing visitors to observe the veterinary checkups and even operations.

A floating pavilion adjacent to the aquarium features sea lions, and harbor seals reside in the outdoor pool on the aquarium's plaza. Some of these seals were found as orphaned pups along the

New England coast and have been cared for by skilled aquarium biologists as part of the Rescue and Rehabilitation Program. Aquarium staff work with whales, dolphins, sea turtles, seals, and others. Whenever possible, these animals are released back into the wild.

Other research programs include working to preserve the endangered red-bellied turtle species and to help increase the declining population of black-footed penguins. The New England Aquarium also offers whale-watching tours and a variety of outreach programs. To maintain such a range of exhibits and programs, the New England Aquarium relies on the skills and experience of a range of professionals.

Steven Bailey, Curator of Fishes

Steven Bailey received his bachelor's degree in zoology from Wilkes University in Wilkes-Barre, Pennsylvania, and completed substantial work toward a master's degree in ichthyology at Northeastern University in Boston. When a full-time job as an aquarist came up at the aquarium, he jumped at the chance, moving up the ranks to his current position.

Bailey spent much of his academic career preparing for aquatic-oriented work, initially looking for a diving job of some sort. His father had been immersed in forestry and took Bailey and his younger brother diving during summer trips to Maine. "The perfect way to start," Bailey says.

During graduate school he volunteered with the National Marine Fishery Service and spent time as a professional collector, collecting specimens used for biomedical research. Few people with his credentials had a great deal of diving experience in the mideighties, and a mentor of his recommended him for a full-time aquarist job at the New England Aquarium, where he was also volunteering at the time.

Starting out as an aquarist, he advanced over thirteen years to senior aquarist and then, as he puts it, "moved out of the best job in the building to the most aggravating job. . . . Somehow I bypassed that last supervisor step and went from senior aquarist to . . . curator of fishes."

Management Duties. Bailey is responsible for everything but the marine mammals—all the fishes, invertebrates, reptiles, amphibians, birds, and plants. That includes two of the biggest exhibits, the Caribbean Coral Reef Exhibit and the penguin colony, which is at the base of the coral reef tank. He also manages twenty-four people: nineteen aquarists at different levels and four supervisors, the equivalent of assistant curators. A curatorial associate under his charge keeps track of everything from how much frozen food they feed the fishes to making sure all of their permits are up to date. The associate "pitches in wherever she can," he says, "whether that's on a collecting trip or helping to haul a five-hundred-pound turtle out of an exhibit for a blood sampling."

Along with managing staff comes hiring, a process Bailey calls incredibly selective. For every job opening advertised, Bailey says the aquarium receives at least two hundred resumes. Serious candidates must have diving experience as well as a degree, preferably in animal biology, but possibly in a related major such as environmental science or general biology. After overall qualifications, Bailey looks at potential candidates' work ethic. If they have worked for a veterinarian, at a pet store, or run their own grooming business, for example, he can infer that those people are willing to do whatever it takes to remain in contact with animals. If that ethic doesn't come through on a resume, candidates should count on emphasizing it in a cover letter or demonstrating it in an interview.

Being interested in fishes is obviously a plus. Maybe someone has been a home hobbyist for years and can go on at length about the animals they've had in that time. Or they've developed the passion from a stimulating course in college. Some candidates experience epiphanies during fieldwork.

Bailey laments that his curatorial responsibilities keep him away from the day-to-day relationships with the animals that he once had. He deals primarily with budget and personnel issues and cites college courses in accounting and abnormal psychology—courses he did not take—as beneficial to a manager in his shoes. "The positive aspects of this job are much different than what initially attracted me to the field," he says. "I don't get out and go collecting that often, but I do manage to get a fair amount of satisfaction and sense of accomplishment from being involved in the design and exhibit construction end of things. We, as a group—the husbandry folks, the design department, education, research—get together to plot our course."

Curating on the Ground. Bailey's group oversees eighty to ninety exhibits, each of which requires an enormous amount of attention, from making sure the animals have balanced diets to aesthetics, what Bailey summarizes as the three Ws—the windows, the walls, the water. "They all have to be clean and aesthetically appealing so that when folks come to visit us, they are immediately assured that professionals are managing the animals," he says. "They spend money to visit here, and they should get a good return on their dollar."

Bailey calls stewardship a major part of an aquarium's reason for existence. Because of all the endangered and threatened marine species, and of course their habitats, the long-term survival of these animals hinges upon the success of aquariums. Taken as such, aquariums, like zoos, function as restocking facilities for wild populations. But the mission also has a surprising amount of overlap with the educational component. In the Medical Center Exhibit, for example, visitors get to see the ins and outs of rehabilitation and examinations firsthand.

One aquarist at the New England Aquarium travels to the Amazon each year to run an ecotourism operation where people pay to help assess biodiversity and explore the habitats with a knowledgeable guide. The money it generates supports Brazilian researchers working to protect those same animals and habitats. "There is no substitute for seeing the real thing," Bailey says. The most popular fish for home aquariums, called the cardinal tetra, comes from the Rio Negro river system, part of the Amazon basin. The tetra's marketability makes its habitat one of the most intact portions of the Amazon basin because the forty to fifty thousand people who live there derive a living from sale of the fish, and they therefore don't depend on destructive farming practices or the hunting of endangered animals to survive.

Advice from Steven Bailey. Becoming an aquarist, particularly at a top-tier facility such as the New England Aquarium, doesn't happen overnight. Bailey says few of his staff were hired the first time around and usually not right out of college. Persevere, and take time to develop a broad set of skills. Volunteer, take related jobs, pursue further courses of study. The job requires construction and tool skills and a person who knows his or her way around the literature or who can at least find the information necessary to answer a question or solve a problem.

That true connection with the animals and to the field must be able to sustain a person through what can become routine and often repetitive work. "Not all of these animals have the excitement or energy of, say, a panda or a killer whale," Bailey says. "Those are animals that get a lot of attention from the public, but nevertheless an animal is an animal, and whether you are talking about a minnow that is abundant five miles away from this institution or one of those more glamourous animals, such as the California sea otter, the bottom line is still the same. They depend on you, and you are responsible for their well-being.

"It can get very old for some people. For other people it's a Zen experience. They put it into perspective; they are able to be at peace with the incredible amount of responsibility they have for all of these animals."

Heather Urquhart, Senior Aquarist

Heather Urquhart is a diving aquarist in the Fishes Department at the New England Aquarium in Boston. She is also a certified advanced scuba diver and has been working at the aquarium since 1989.

"I have always known that I wanted to work with animals," Urquhart says. Initially she expected that might be as a veterinarian or a zookeeper. But she also grew up on the ocean, and after seeing Jacques Cousteau on TV, she decided she wanted to work with marine animals. "I've always been an ocean buff," she says. "When I was a kid, I was always the one without a suntan. I always had my mask and snorkel on."

Urquhart earned a bachelor's degree in biology from Salem State College, concentrating on marine biology and picking up a minor in chemistry. She had grown up in the Boston area, and when she started school in Salem, which is nearby, she learned about the aquarium's volunteer program. Urquhart lumped all her classes into Mondays, Wednesdays, and Fridays and began volunteering at the penguin exhibit on Tuesdays and Thursdays. Once she graduated, she worked a couple of other jobs, with an environmental consulting firm and in quality control for seafood, but she continually applied for jobs at the New England Aquarium when they became available. Eventually they called her in for an interview, and on the strength of a recommendation from her six-month stint as a volunteer, they hired her. "Before I got my job here, I thought for sure I'd be going on for a master's, but once you get involved with your work doing something that you love, it's hard to break away to go back to school," she says.

She's been at the aquarium since, first as an aquarist-in-training, then a full-fledged aquarist, and finally as a senior aquarist in the fishes department, where she works with the penguins.

On the Job. Urquhart dives up to five times a day to feed and examine the fish and also to clean and maintain the exhibit. She takes care of both the penguin colony and the giant ocean tank. If there are enough people available, staff members rotate so that an aquarist doesn't have to go in every day. There's plenty of work to go around. "The penguin exhibit has a 131,000-gallon tank, and we need seven staff people to maintain both exhibits, plus we have volunteers to help us seven days a week," Urquhart says. They don't dive in the penguin exhibit, but they do have to don wet suits to tolerate fifty-five-degree water up to their chests. "There are days you just don't feel like getting wet, but you grin and bear it," she says. "If one of us is ill with a bad cold or the flu, then we try to accommodate each other, but even then I've gone in. There was no choice. The fish have to be fed."

The job is highly physical, then, and not only because of the diving. There's putting on the suit and diving equipment, ascending and descending the four flights of stairs necessary to get in and out of the penguin exhibit, and lugging the two fifteen-pound buckets of fish for feeding.

Urquhart says she enjoys the interaction with the animals the most. "No matter what kind of aggravating day you might be having, when you are working with the animals, it all seems not to matter so much," she says. None of the penguins is trained, though they are teachable. The aquarium aims to show visitors what the birds are like in their natural environment as much as possible. Some have been partially raised by hand, however, and those are more accustomed to human interaction. Aquarists will use them to do "animal interviews," where they place the birds in a separate enclosure closer to the public (but still not within reach). They don't mind being in the spotlight as much.

Urquhart herself has hand raised a fair number of penguins, from egg to adult. She calls it a wonderful experience. "They imprint on you, and they know my voice and will come to me," she says. As they grow into adults and begin to seek mates, the penguins lose interest in people. The birds are banded, so staff can keep track of who's who and monitor their mating habits to prevent inbreeding. (The aquarium has a full genealogy for each penguin as well as food records, medical records, and records of molting patterns.)

The genealogical information can be critical. More than half of penguin species worldwide are threatened or endangered, so increasing numbers of captive birds and maintaining as much genetic diversity as possible are paramount to preserving the species. Penguin pairs that aren't getting along or would result in inbreeding get separated and introduced to better matches.

The exhibit contains two penguin species: the rockhopper, which in the wild inhabits the small islands between Antarctica and South America, Africa, and Australia; and the African penguin, an endangered species living along the coast of southern Africa and whose numbers have dwindled for a variety of reasons, including historical human destruction of cliffside nests, overfishing of the penguins' main prey, and oil spills on the African cape. Urquhart has visited South Africa several times and returned with a better understanding of the African penguins' plight and passes that knowledge on to guests at the New England Aquarium. The aquarium contributes to rehabilitation organizations that are helping oiled penguins in South Africa. Its staff also travels up and down the East Coast collecting fish and invertebrates for the exhibits and runs a collecting trip twice a year to the Bahamas to collect for the Caribbean Coral Reef Exhibit.

Risks of the Trade. Sharks rove the Caribbean exhibit that Urquhart and her fellow aquarists dive in, but she evinces more concern about the aquarium's smaller inhabitants. "I think people have a lot of misconceptions about sharks," she says. "People aren't on a shark's menu, and a lot of times attacks are the result of mistaken identity." Instead, it's the inch-long damselfish, often protecting their nests, that divers must heed. Urquhart says she's been bitten by damselfish many times, though nothing that inflicted permanent damage, and also by penguins. "They aren't trying to be mean, but you're down there feeding them and handling them, and they aren't tame animals," she says. With the amount of interaction aquarists have with the animals, birds and fish alike, they're bound to end up getting nips and bites sooner or later. But Urquhart isn't overly concerned, saying that the staffers dealing with stranded animals, such as sick seals, probably have to worry more about being bitten or harmed than an aquarium diver.

Advice from Heather Urquhart. Volunteer, volunteer, volunteer. The vast majority of the people working at the New England Aquarium formerly volunteered there. Not only will the people who work at the institution get to know your work, but you'll get an idea of what you'd be getting into. "The glamorous part is that you get to work with a lot of cute baby animals," she says. "But the nonglamorous part is all that other stuff of being in a wet suit all day long, in cold water, and smelling like fish by the end of the day. Ninety percent of working with animals is cleaning up after them. It's not for everyone."

Urquhart advises not specializing too early. A degree in biology or zoology would be good for someone in her job. Once you've investigated your alternatives and volunteered at a few places, you can better decide what area to focus on. You might decide you'd rather work in a lab or in education.

Jenny Montague, Assistant Curator/ Animal Trainer

Jenny Montague is assistant curator in the Marine Mammals Department at the New England Aquarium, a position equivalent to supervisor in the Fishes Department. While still in high school, she worked as a landscaper at Marine World/Africa USA in Vallejo, California, a combination marine park and zoo. Desperate to carve out a career working with marine mammals, she'd arrive at Marine World at five in the morning to landscape, then return after school and work until dark.

Right after her high school graduation, Marine World hired her as an assistant trainer in the Marine Mammals Department. (She also attended community college.) After eight years, she left her job as senior trainer and show manager at Marine World to work in Boston as the supervisor of marine mammals at the New England Aquarium. The curator there had worked briefly at Marine World on a research project and so knew Montague. "When the supervisor position opened, she called me, and I said yes pretty quickly," Montague recalls. "I was ready for a change." A phone interview sealed the deal, and she has been with the New England Aquarium since.

"One of the nicest things about the job is that you never run out of ideas, and you're able to try them out," she says. "It's different every day." That's also a roundabout way of saying the hours are inconsistent. The staff typically works four ten-hour days, but with the aquarium open seven days a week and the unpredictable nature of animals, something always arises that disturbs the routine. "That," Montague says, "might be a good thing."

On the Job. As an assistant curator, Montague supervises eight people who train and monitor the animals and present them to the public. They work with the colony of resident marine mammals, including Atlantic harbor seals, California sea lions, and California sea otters. The shows, four to seven of them a day, are conducted indoors and are divided amongst the staff. Montague herself personally emcees eight to ten shows per week, and three or four staffers might pitch in on a show if they're working with multiple animals. The idea is to present the animals' backgrounds, natural histories, and the conservation issues surrounding them in an entertaining way.

"When people can get close to live animals, it makes an incredible impression on them," she says. Audience members are an active part of the shows, not merely spectators. In one instance, trainers asked for suggestions on how to make the ocean a safer place for the animals, and those who had interesting ideas got to meet the sea lion "headlining" the show and give him a kiss. All different levels of trainers participate, too, from the assistant trainers to assistant curators. They talk about the animals' physiology and biology and the training techniques the staff members use. They demonstrate some of the medical care involved, such as brushing the animals' teeth and listening to heartbeats with a stethoscope. The animals open their mouths to let the veterinarians look down their throats or sit still for an eye exam. "The training is for the medical care of the animals, but it's also for mental stimulation," Montague says. "We find that, like anyone, if they are stimulated mentally and physically, they are much happier and healthier animals than if they are just left alone."

Trainers regularly weigh the animals and assess their diets. The fish used for food is sent out for analysis so the staff knows exactly how many calories and how many grams of fat are in each kind of fish. That information then gets compared to a formula to calculate the proper amount of food based on the animal's age and weight.

Animal Training. Montague says that every animal has its own personality and, therefore, its own learning curve and approach to training. "With some animals, you can work on a particular behavior for half an hour and do several repeats, and then they make a step," she says. "We have one sea lion that if we repeat things over and over and lead him slowly through little steps, he'll never forget what you've taught him. Another one gets bored very easily, and he starts to add in his own special flair. We spend more time retraining him than training him to get rid of all his extraneous stuff. But he's a howl, one of the most fun sea lions to work with."

Each animal usually has two primary trainers in order to cover the entire workday. Those primary trainers work as a team and are responsible for deciding what the animals are going to learn, who will train them, and what methods the trainers will use. The trainers keep records of all the advances the animals make and what new steps they've accomplished.

Trainers use three different methods. The most widely used is operant conditioning, breaking a behavior into small steps and reinforcing each step with rewards, such as food or touch. Operant conditioning relies on repetition and the animal's association of a certain behavior with positive outcomes.

A second common method is innovative training, which is just what it sounds like. Once an animal has a solid understanding of operant conditioning, trainers give them an arbitrary signal, such as crossing their arms across their chest. The animal won't have seen this signal before but might associate it with a similar signal, or invent its own action to gain the reward. At first the trainers will reward behavior corresponding to an existing signal, but eventually they'll reward only new behaviors. "You spend a lot of time trying to find what the animals enjoy," Montague says. "Some like particular toys, others like things like ice cubes. So, for example, after the signal, they might give a salute. We'll reward it, and then . . . they figure that if they do it again, they'll be rewarded again. But the next time we don't reinforce the salute. You can get a curious look from them at that point. We'll give the signal again, and, if the salute doesn't work yet again, they'll start to offer something else, whether it's a look in another direction, or moving their whiskers forward in a curious questioning look."

Trainers reward these subsequent experimental behaviors, which encourages the animals to invent some ever more clever actions. The idea is to stimulate their creativity based on things they already like to do. It also gives the training staff some ideas. "Our sea lion Zack used to carry some rings around on his flippers and slap them at the same time," she says. "He would have all his flippers going and then he'd roll over."

The third training method is mimicry. Trainers ask the animals to focus on them and copy what they do. The animals already mimic the trainers to some extent, such as turning around in a circle, hopping up, or making a sound, so the trainers build on that ability to teach new tricks. "It's really fun," Montague says, "and the benefit is that it gives them a whole different focus. They have to watch our whole bodies completely, instead of just the usual hand gestures."

The amount of time trainers spend on teaching a trick depends on how much the animals enjoy it and are willing to cooperate. While the tricks do serve a purpose in endearing the animals to the audience, the training display isn't a circus. Often the tricks showcase the natural behavior and talents of the animals, such as porpoising—bursting out of the water in an arc during fast swimming, a maneuver that in the wild allows dolphins and certain whales to increase speed by reducing the drag of water. Trainers simply teach the dolphins to porpoise on command.

Sometimes the trainers at the New England Aquarium work with the sea lions at the same time as the harbor seals. "There is a major difference in speed between the two," Montague says. "The sea lions are much faster. The seals slug along on their bellies; they're not the most graceful creatures on land." Trainers have worked with the sea lions to gallop, demonstrating just how fast they can get around over ground.

Finally, the trainers get the animals to accommodate specialized handling for research purposes. When the aquarium started a hearing study, for example, the trainers began teaching the animals to tolerate wearing headphones, then to respond to sound cues.

Advice from Jenny Montague. Like Heather Urquhart, Montague strongly recommends volunteering in a facility where you think you'd enjoy working. This shows managers what it might be like to work with you full-time, and it also allows you to experience everything that goes into training work behind the scenes. "A lot of times folks come and see animal shows and they think that's all there is to it," Montague says. "But it isn't. We're up to our elbows in sinks full of dead fish all the time." Also keep in mind that every facility will have a different style, so volunteering at more than one place (though not necessarily at one time!) can provide you with a broader view.

At one time, colleges didn't offer programs on marine-animal training. If you were interested in animal behavior, you worked with pigeons and rats. Montague's experience, tellingly, came from volunteering and working hands-on at Marine World. Today's students have more academic options for marine-animal training. "My advice would be to find any one of the schools that works with animal behavior," she says. "The interesting part of this job is that there are different academic subjects that can help you, such as psychology, animal behavior, and some zoology." Two of the best-known training schools are Moorpark College's Exotic Animal Training and Management program in Moorpark, California (www.moorpark.cc.ca.us/~eatm) and the University of California at Santa Cruz, which runs the Long Marine Lab and its Pinniped Research in Cognition & Sensory Systems program (http://pinnipedlab.ucsc.edu).

Trainers recommend not specializing in one area too quickly. Start out with a broad focus and hone in as you gain more experience. Many aspiring trainers mistakenly believe that earning a degree in marine biology is the appropriate track to get into training. It's not. Consider instead a degree in biology or zoology with internships or research projects involving animal training—or, of course, a school dedicated to training if you're positive that's what you want to do.

CHAPTER TWO

At Attention with the Military

Maintaining a strong national defense encompasses such diverse activities as running a hospital, commanding a tank crew, programming computers, operating a nuclear reactor, and repairing a helicopter. The military's occupational diversity provides educational opportunities and work experience in literally hundreds of occupations.

Military personnel hold managerial and administrative jobs; professional, technical, and clerical jobs; construction jobs; electrical and electronics jobs; mechanical and repair jobs; and many others. There are hundreds of basic and advanced military occupational specialties for enlisted personnel and almost as many for officers. Often these occupational specialties have civilian counterparts. Three branches of the armed forces, both in the United States and Canada, offer aquatic types the chance to be at sea: the U.S. Navy, U.S. Coast Guard, and U.S. Marine Corps; and the Canadian Navy, Canadian Coast Guard, and Canada Command.

Military Life

Military life is more regimented than civilian life, and one who enlists must be willing to accept the discipline. It is important to remember that signing an enlistment contract obligates you to serve for a specified period of time. Dress and grooming requirements are stringent, and rigid formalities govern many aspects of daily life. For instance, officers and enlisted personnel do not socialize together, and commissioned officers are saluted and addressed as "sir" or "ma'am." These and other rules encourage respect for superiors whose commands must be obeyed immediately and without question.

The needs of the military always come first. As a result, hours and working conditions can vary substantially. However, most military personnel not deployed on a mission usually work eight hours a day, five days a week. At sea they might work twelve hours a day, seven days a week.

While off duty, military personnel usually do not wear their uniforms and are free to participate in family and recreational activities like most civilians. Some assignments, however, require night and weekend work or require people to be on call at all hours. Depending on the service, assignments may require long periods at sea, sometimes in cramped quarters, or lengthy overseas assignments in countries offering few amenities. Some personnel serve tours in isolated parts of the world, where they are subject to extreme cold or heat and the possibility of hostilities breaking out at any time. Others, such as sailors on carrier flight-deck duty, have jobs that are hazardous even in noncombat situations.

During wartime, many military personnel engage in combat and find themselves in life-or-death situations. They rely on countless hours of training to produce teamwork that is critical to the success of operations and to protecting the lives of the individuals in their unit. Rapidly advancing military technology has made warfare more precise and lethal, further increasing the need for specialized training.

Noncombatants may also face danger if their duties bring them close to a combat zone. Even in peacetime, most members of the combat branches of the military participate in hazardous training activities.

Ship and air crews travel extensively, while others in the military are stationed at bases throughout the country or overseas. Military personnel are usually transferred to new duty stations every few years.

Military personnel do enjoy more job security than their civilian counterparts. Satisfactory job performance generally assures military personnel steady employment and a raft of sizable benefits: full medical and dental care, advanced training, educational benefits, discounted travel, extensive vacation, and life insurance. Other basics, such as meals, clothing, and living quarters, are provided.

A Few Military Statistics

About 1.5 million people are on active duty in the U.S. armed forces:

Navy	375,000
Marine Corps	180,000
Coast Guard	40,000
Army	500,000
Air Force	358,000

Women account for 15 percent of active-duty personnel in combined U.S. forces, with the air force having the highest number and marines by far the lowest. Canada, whose military has a modified, unified structure, has about sixty-four thousand regular personnel, 11 percent of which are women.

Military personnel are stationed throughout North America and in many countries around the world. In the United States, California, Texas, North Carolina, and Virginia account for more than one in three military jobs. About 249,000 U.S. military are stationed outside the United States, with more than 100,000 in Europe (mainly Germany) and in the Western Pacific.

How to Qualify

As it has since 1973, the U.S. military meets its personnel requirements through volunteers. Enlisted members must enter a legal agreement called an enlistment contract, which usually involves a commitment to eight years of service. Depending on the terms of the contract, two to six years are spent on active duty, the balance in the reserves. The enlistment contract obligates the military to provide the agreed-upon options—job, rating, pay, cash bonuses for enlistment in certain occupations, medical and other benefits, occupational training, and continuing education. In return, enlisted personnel must serve satisfactorily for the specified period of time.

Requirements for each service vary, but certain qualifications for enlistment are common to all branches. An enlistee must be between the ages of seventeen and thirty-five, must be a U.S. citizen or immigrant alien holding permanent resident status, must not have a felony record, and must possess a birth certificate. Applicants who are seventeen must have the consent of a parent or legal guardian before entering the service.

Applicants must pass both a written examination—the Armed Services Vocational Aptitude Battery—and meet certain minimum physical standards such as height, weight, vision, and overall health. All branches prefer high school graduation or its equivalent and require it for certain enlistment options. Single parents are generally not eligible to enlist.

In the Canadian Forces, an enlistee must be a Canadian citizen or, in exceptional circumstances, a permanent resident of Canada and must also be at least seventeen years of age. Junior-level military college applicants and reservists may be sixteen. Educational standards vary depending on the position, from completion of tenth grade to holding a university degree. Applicants must also pass physical and aptitude tests before being accepted.

People thinking about enlisting in the military should learn as much as they can about military life before making a decision. This is especially important if you are thinking about making the military a career. Speaking to friends and relatives with military experience is a good idea. Determine what the military can offer you and what it will expect in return. Then talk to a recruiter, who can determine whether you qualify for enlistment, explain the various enlistment options, and tell you which military occupational specialties currently have openings for trainees. Bear in mind that the recruiter's job is to recruit promising young men and women into the military, so the information he or she gives you is likely to stress the positive aspects of military life.

Ask the recruiter to assess your chances of being accepted for training in the occupation or occupations of your choice or, better still, take the aptitude exam to see how well you score. The military uses the aptitude exam as a placement exam, and test scores largely determine an individual's chances of being accepted into a particular training program. Selection for a particular type of training depends on the needs of the service, general and technical aptitudes, and personal preference. Because all prospective recruits are required to take the exam, those who do so before committing themselves to enlist have the advantage of knowing in advance whether they stand a good chance of being accepted for training in a particular specialty. Many high schools offer the exam as an easy way for students to explore the possibility of a military career, and the test also provides insight into career areas where the student has demonstrated aptitude and interest.

The Enlistment Contract

If you decide to join the military, the next step is to pass the physical examination and then enter into the enlistment contract. This involves choosing, qualifying, and agreeing on a number of enlistment options such as length of active-duty time, which may vary according to the enlistment option. (Most active-duty programs have enlistment options ranging from three to six years, although there are some two-year programs.) The contract will also state the date of enlistment and other options such as bonuses and types of training to be received. If the service is unable to fulfill its part of the contract, such as providing a certain kind of training, the contract may become null and void.

U.S. and Canadian services also offer a delayed-entry program by which an enlistee can delay entry into active duty for up to one year. High school students can enlist during their senior year and enter service after graduation. Others choose this program because the job training they desire is not currently available but will be within the coming year or because they need time to arrange personal affairs.

Women are eligible to enter almost all military specialties. Although many women serve in medical and administrative support positions, they also work as mechanics, missile-maintenance technicians, heavy-equipment operators, fighter pilots, and intelligence officers. Only occupations involving a high probability of direct exposure to combat are excluded—for example, the artillery and infantry branches of the army.

People planning to apply the skills gained through military training to a civilian career should look into several things before selecting a military occupation. First, they should determine how good the prospects are for civilian employment in jobs related to the military specialties that interest them. Second, they should know the prerequisites for the related civilian jobs. Many occupations require a license, certification, or a minimum level of education. In such cases, it is important to determine whether military training is sufficient to enter the civilian equivalent or, if not, what additional training will be required.

Following enlistment, new members of the armed forces undergo recruit training. Better known as basic training or boot camp, recruit training provides a six- to eleven-week introduction to military life with courses in health, first aid, and military skills and protocol. Days and nights are carefully structured and include rigorous physical exercises designed to improve strength and endurance.

Following basic training, most recruits take additional training at technical schools that prepare them for a particular military occupational specialty. The formal training period generally lasts from ten to twenty weeks, although training for certain more technical occupations—nuclear power plant operator, for example—may take as much as one year. Recruits who are not assigned to classroom instruction receive on-the-job training at the first duty assignment.

Many service people earn college credit for the technical training they receive on duty, which, combined with off-duty courses, can lead to an associate's degree through community college programs such as the Community College of the Air Force.

In addition to on-duty training, military personnel may choose from a variety of educational programs. Most military installations have tuition-assistance programs for people wishing to take courses during off-duty hours. These may be correspondence courses or degree programs offered by local colleges or universities. Tuition assistance for U.S. military pays up to 100 percent of college costs (currently $1,075 per month for full-time). Canadian Forces also may cover the entire cost of an education depending on the position and degree program. See www.forces.ca/v3/engraph/resources/payandbenefits_en.aspx for information. Also available are courses designed to help service personnel earn high school equivalency diplomas. Each service branch provides opportunities for full-time study to a limited number of exceptional applicants. Military personnel accepted into these highly competitive programs receive full pay, allowances, tuition, and related fees. In return, they must agree to serve an additional amount of time in the service. Other very selective programs enable enlisted personnel to qualify as commissioned officers through additional military training.

U.S. Officer Training

Officer training in the U.S. armed forces is provided through federal service academies, the Reserve Officers Training Corps (ROTC), Officer Candidate School (OCS) or Officer Training School (OTS), the National Guard (State Officer Candidate

School programs), the Uniformed Services University of Health Sciences (USUHS), and other programs. All are very selective and are good options for those wishing to begin a military career. Federal service academies provide a four-year college program leading to a bachelor of science degree. The midshipman or cadet is provided free room and board, tuition, medical care, and a monthly allowance. Graduates receive regular or reserve commissions and have a five-year active duty obligation, longer if entering flight training.

To become a candidate for appointment as a cadet or midshipman in one of the service academies, most applicants obtain a nomination from an authorized source, usually a member of Congress. (Candidates do not need to know a member of Congress personally to request a nomination.) Nominees must have an academic record of the requisite quality, college aptitude test scores above an established minimum, and recommendations from teachers or school officials; they must also pass a medical examination. Appointments are made from the list of eligible nominees.

Appointments to the Coast Guard Academy are made strictly on a competitive basis. A nomination is not required.

ROTC programs train students in army, navy and marines, and air force units (organized under the Air Force Officer Accession and Training Schools, AFOATS) at participating colleges and universities. (Find programs at www.goarmy.com/rotc/find _schools.jsp, www.nrotc.navy.mil/colleges.cfm, and www.afrotc .com/colleges/detLocator.php.) Trainees take two to five hours of military instruction a week in addition to regular college courses. After graduation, they may serve as officers on active duty for a stipulated period of time, at the convenience of the service. Some may serve their obligation in the reserves or guard. In the last two years of an ROTC program, students receive a monthly allowance while attending school and additional pay for summer training. ROTC scholarships for two, three, and four years are available on a competitive basis. All scholarships pay for tuition and have allowances for subsistence, textbooks, supplies, and other fees.

College graduates can earn commissions in the armed forces through OCS or OTS programs in the army, navy, air force, marines, coast guard, and national guard. These officers must serve their obligation on active duty. People with training in certain health professions may qualify for direct appointment as officers. In the case of health professions students, financial assistance and internship opportunities are available from the military in return for specified periods of military service. Prospective medical students can apply to the Uniformed Services University of Health Sciences, which offers free tuition in a program leading to an M.D. degree. In return, graduates must serve for seven years in either the military or the Public Health Service. Direct appointments also are available for those qualified to serve in other special duties, such as the judge advocate general (legal) or chaplain corps.

Flight training is available to commissioned officers in each branch of the armed forces. In addition, the army has a direct enlistment option to become a warrant officer aviator.

Each service has different criteria for promoting personnel. Generally, the first few promotions for both enlisted and officer personnel come easily; subsequent promotions are much more competitive. Criteria for promotion may include time in service and grade, job performance, a fitness report (supervisor's recommendation), and written examinations. Those who are passed over for promotion several times generally must leave the military.

Canadian Officer Training

Officer candidates in the Canadian military attend the Royal Military College (RMC) in Kingston, Ontario. The most common entry method is via the Regular Officer Training Plan (ROTP), where students attend the RMC full-time and, upon graduation, accept commissions as officers in the Canadian Forces for at least five years. In return, the Department of National Defence covers educational costs and pays students a monthly stipend, deducting housing and meal costs from it.

Under the Reserve entry Training Plan (ReTP), cadets receive the same training and education as ROTP cadets but must pay tuition and a variety of fees. ReTP cadets then receive commissions in the Primary Reserve after graduation, but they could transfer to the regular component of the Canadian Forces.

Those who are already enlisted in the Canadian Forces and want to become officers can apply to the RMC through the University Training Plan—Non-Commissioned Members (UTPNCM). Members with sufficient previous academic experience might receive advanced standing rather than beginning as first-year cadets, and they also might receive certain allowances, such as for marriage, that traditional officer candidates would not. UTPNCM cadets receive commissions and promotions upon graduation.

Regardless of the mode of entry, programs are interdisciplinary, and students graduate with fluency in both French and English. If you find during your first year that undertaking an officer commission was a mistake, you can request release with no further obligation. If you're considering a commission with the Canadian Forces, contact a recruiting center (www.recruiting.forces.gc.ca) at least a year before you apply to assess your career options and discuss ways to improve your chances of receiving a commission.

Students high school age or younger who want to get a jump on a military career should consider joining Canada's Sea Cadets, Army Cadets, or Air Cadets, which are federally sponsored programs designed for twelve- to eighteen-year-olds that promote teamwork, leadership, and citizenship through quasimilitary activities. (See www.cadets.ca for more information.)

Career Outlook

The U.S. military faces chronic recruiting shortages among both enlisted personnel and officers. About 170,000 personnel must be recruited each year just to replace those who retire or otherwise fulfill their commitments. While this does not mean the military will take just anybody, its innovative recruitment programs should make joining more attractive and consistent with the lifestyles that younger workers, particularly men, have.

Educational requirements will continue to rise as military jobs become more technical and complex, but many military programs now offer training customized to individual career goals, easing the transition from military to private sector work when the time comes.

Although Canada's fighting force is much smaller, it confronts similar challenges in maintaining its ranks and has mounted an ambitious plan to both offset downturns from attrition and retirement and meet new commitments for increased staffing levels. The Canadian Forces currently fall well below the established benchmark of one hundred thousand regular and reserve members, which itself is a steep drop-off from the World War II era. Serious candidates should expect to find a well-earned place in the future of Canada's military.

Salaries, Allowances, and Benefits

Military paychecks are infamous for being smaller than their civilian counterparts, but they do come with a complement of related benefits that civilian jobs can't match, such as housing allowances, meals, hardship duty pay, and tax advantages. See the website at www.todaysmilitary.com/app/tm/get/compensation for U.S. military compensation rates and www.dod.mil/militarypay/pay/bp/index.html for current information on base salaries and raises. For Canadian military rates, see the website of the Directorate of Pay Policy and Development at www.forces.gc.ca/dgcb/dppd/engraph/home_e.asp.

In addition to basic pay, military personnel receive free room and board (or a tax-free housing and subsistence allowance), medical and dental care, a military clothing allowance, military supermarket and department store shopping privileges, thirty days of paid vacation a year, and travel opportunities.

Other allowances are paid for foreign duty, hazardous duty, submarine and flight duty, and employment as a medical officer. Athletic and other recreational facilities such as libraries, gymnasiums, tennis courts, golf courses, bowling centers, and movies are available on many military installations. Military personnel are eligible for retirement benefits after twenty years of service.

Veterans' Benefits

In the United States, the Veterans Administration (VA) provides numerous benefits to those who have served at least two years in the armed forces. Veterans are eligible for free care in VA hospitals for all service-connected disabilities regardless of time served; those with other medical problems are eligible for free VA care if they are unable to pay the cost of hospitalization elsewhere. Admission to a VA medical center depends on the availability of beds. Veterans are also eligible for certain loans, including home loans. Regardless of health, a veteran can convert a military life insurance policy to an individual policy with any participating company in the veteran's state of residence. Job counseling, testing, and placement services are also available.

Veterans who take advantage of the Montgomery GI Bill receive educational benefits. Under this program, the Veterans Administration pays for up to thirty-six months of higher education or career training for veterans who served at least three years in the military. Veterans who served in active duty are eligible for more than $36,000 in benefits, while reservists could see about one-third as much. See www.gibill.com for general information about the program and www.gibill.va.gov/GI_Bill_Info/rates.htm for current benefit levels from the VA.

The Canadian Forces offer a Regular Force education reimbursement (ER) and a Primary Reserve education reimbursement for current members. If the degree is in line with the interests of the Canadian Forces, it will reimburse 100 percent of tuition for eligible members where costs aren't already covered under other programs. The Skills Completion Program offers up to $5,000 to Regular Force members trying to transfer their skills to the private sector, especially noncommissioned members in occupations with no direct civilian application. The program can apply for up to two years after release from the military. See www.forces.ca/v3/engraph/resources/payandbenefits_en.aspx for information on educational benefits.

What It's Really Like

With so many different career opportunities offered through branches of the military, it would be impossible to provide you with a representative sample of firsthand accounts in all the various fields. Make every effort to talk to people in the service you're interested in to get a clearer picture of whether it's the right choice for you. The two profiles here, both from the U.S. Navy, are atypical of military work in that they're about communications positions. Both men have spent significant time at sea, however, and they do possess great insight into military seafaring. Canadian sailors could expect a similar experience.

James Roman Stilipec, U.S. Navy Journalist

Petty Officer Third Class James Roman Stilipec hails from North Pole, Alaska. As a navy journalist, he trained in Maryland and Virginia before working ashore in Spain and on the USS *Carl Vinson*, one of just thirteen aircraft carriers navywide. Stilipec was drawn to the navy through a combination of interest in ships and naval aviation, family history, and dissatisfaction with his career at the time. Selling women's shoes at JC Penney two years out of high school, Stilipec decided there had to be something better to do. Around that time, he received a letter from the navy encouraging him to enlist, and he responded by sending back a form with the programs and areas that appealed to him.

"Before I joined the navy, I never really saw the point of the military," Stilipec confesses. "I figured the world would be at peace in a few decades, and the military wasn't that necessary." But his father had been in the navy in the seventies and had a positive experience, and, as a child, sailing and aviation had intrigued Stilipec. He flew to Anchorage to take a military equivalence exam and scored very high. Suddenly all sorts of avenues seemed open to him. He had long wanted to write creatively, leaning toward fiction in secondary school and stockpiling tons of ideas for stories. He asked the navy for something in communications, which was more independent and creative than many duties he might have chosen.

Early Training. Even before going through boot camp, Stilipec attended the Defense Information School (DINFOS) in Fort Meade, Maryland, to complete preliminary journalism and communications classes. The school teaches print and broadcast journalism, basic photography, and public affairs to all five military branches: navy, army, air force, marines, and coast guard. This took three months and included a final project—a newspaper produced by the entire class. A DINFOS broadcasting course taught him basic announcing skills, electronic news gathering, radio broadcasting, and television studio skills. He graduated from the course on his twentieth birthday.

His first assignment came at the Naval Media Center Broadcast Detachment in Rota, Spain. "I'd never been out of the United States in my life, let alone overseas, so it was quite a nerve-wracking experience for me," he says. But, "when I arrived, I found my coworkers to be friendly and more than willing to help me out. One of them even went through the print journalism course with me, so it was nice to have a familiar face." In Spain he became a jack-of-all-trades: handling cable TV programming for the base, shooting and producing news stories for five- to ten-minute newscasts, anchoring the newscasts, producing TV and radio commercials, and producing two two-hour radio shows—a country show and a rock-and-roll show. The highly varied work gave him a sound foundation on which to build in subsequent jobs.

Going to Sea. In two years in Spain, Stilipec was able to return home only once. He received no visits from family or friends, and he found himself looking for a post closer to home. Less than halfway through his assignment in Spain, he learned about an opening on the USS *Carl Vinson*, which was homeported in Bremerton, Washington, at the time, as close as he was likely to get to Alaska. "I'd wanted to get on a ship since I joined the navy," he says. "I see ships as the 'real navy,' and the chance to get stationed on one, and a carrier at that, was a dream come true." Stilipec knew he would stretch himself on ship more than he ever could have in Spain. As diverse as his work there had been, it had all been broadcast. On the *Carl Vinson* he would get to do print, radio, TV, and public affairs.

The *Carl Vinson* was like a floating city. There was a post office, power plant, airport, sewer system, lookout peak, cafeteria, 7–Eleven, shopping mall, bank, cable TV, and radio stations. Stilipec soon adjusted to the routine of shipboard life, waking at 6 A.M. to shower, shave, dress, and eat breakfast. At 7:15 he'd muster with his division and have a morning meeting at which his boss would give him daily duties, everything from handling distinguished visitors to touch-up painting a wall. At 7:45 the whole ship would clean for an hour, and at 8:45 he'd begin his professional duties.

Working at sea, he says, is much like working on the shore, except that you work and sleep and play in the same place. "At first it's hard to get used to not being able to leave the ship, but soon you find other ways to entertain yourself in your time off." Reading, working out, and correspondence were popular pastimes. Also the entire ship participated in drills on a regular basis. "One minute you're working on a story, the next you're fighting a fire in a smoke-filled space," he says.

Shipboard Journalism. The length of a workday depends on whether the ship is in port or at sea. In port Stilipec worked a basic seven-to-four day, Monday through Friday. At sea he worked every day from 7 A.M. until anywhere from 6 P.M. to midnight. He dealt with the gamut of public communications, a much more inclusive charge than one might at first realize. Communications officials would escort visitors, provide tours—everything from film crews to generals, CEOs to elementary school classes, he says—publish a daily four-page newsletter while at sea, and administer TV and radio programming.

The ship had a collection of eight hundred movies to run on two shipboard channels, one of which was reserved for training tapes and general information for the crew, for example, and Stilipec produced a two-hour rock-and-roll show each day at noon.

For the newsletter he wrote stories about events on the ship to keep the crew informed. With more than fifty-five hundred crew members, the *Carl Vinson* didn't lack for news to cover. He might profile certain crew members, write about sites at an upcoming port, or offer an inside look at a particular area of the ship. "There are some areas of the ship that some sailors might never visit," Stilipec says.

This on top of monitoring all the training for his division, dealing with ordering and purchasing new items for his division, maintaining the equipment, and keeping his space clean. "I've learned that it is possible to get everything done through proper time management and persistence," he says. "If you're in the middle of something and are sent on an errand, when you get back from that errand, return to what you were doing. Eventually everything will get done. And if you don't have anything to do, ask someone if you can help them out. Everyone else is just as busy as you are, and if you can help them out, then everyone gets the job done faster, and there's more time to relax at the end of the day."

Somewhere in there he also found time to eat lunch, usually at eleven, before his noon radio show, and dinner, at four while he was running errands for the newsletter. Nevertheless, he liked working in journalism and public affairs because of the small division (only seven personnel, compared to other divisions that approach one hundred), the collegiality of his coworkers, and their respect for each other's time, space, and work. "Because we were all journalists and knew what it's like to deal with someone editing your story, we all tended to take criticism very well and were usually willing to listen to a new idea," he says. "Many ideas dealt with story writing or video production, and when the creativity is flowing, great ideas abound."

Upsides and Downsides. Stilipec says he liked getting his stories out to the public, producing an interesting radio show, and knowing that what he did influenced people in one way or another— whether it was a sailor who learned something new about the ship she was on or a high school student who decided to join the navy after a tour of the carrier.

The less pleasant aspects of the job for him were the daily and weekly requirements, like cleaning and preventive maintenance. "I know these things are important," he says, "but that doesn't make them exciting." Along with that were the long hours, the occasional bad interview, and the people who thought working in journalism and public affairs was the easiest job in the world. "Everyone in the Navy works hard in one way or another," he says. "I may not have gotten greasy in my job, but what I did was important, it's time-consuming, and it required plenty of knowledge as well as imagination."

Advice from James Stilipec. "The navy is a great place to start out," he says. "Much of the training is directly transferable to the civilian world. You should get to travel and see things you may have never seen in your life. But it is not for the fainthearted, and it is very different from civilian life. Honor, courage, and commitment are the core values of the navy. If you join, realize in advance that it's not like camp."

David Butts, Master Chief Journalist

David Butts has been in the U.S. Navy since 1976. Now a master chief journalist based in Washington, D.C., he has attended various schools and training programs offered by the navy, such as firefighting, print and broadcast journalism, communications, and others, and served as Chief Petty Officer Third Class James Roman Stilipec's supervisor aboard the USS *Carl Vinson.*

He originally entered the navy for the travel opportunities and educational benefits and chose journalism because of his interest in writing, public speaking, and other communications areas. Like Stilipec, his first training came at the Defense Information School (DINFOS) at Fort Meade, Maryland, where he learned the basics of print and broadcast journalism. While there, he studied public relations theory, writing, photography, layout, and design. He has since returned to DINFOS for intermediate photojournalism school and broadcast station manager's school.

Hands-on Experience. The navy has fulfilled Butts's dream to travel all over the world, sending him to fifteen countries and thirty-two states. He has worked as a newspaper reporter and photojournalist in the Philippines for *Stars and Stripes* and as a news director and executive producer in Korea for the American Forces Network, and he has pulled a tour in the Persian Gulf. He has edited two navywide publications: *LINK,* a professional bulletin for all enlisted personnel in the navy, and *All Hands,* a monthly feature and news magazine about the navy and its people. Both have print runs of nearly one hundred thousand.

The jobs, marked by a transient lifestyle away from family and friends, can be grueling. "Every two or three years, I transferred to a new job and a new place," Butts says, "sometimes working pretty standard forty-hour weeks, but many jobs required nearly twice that."

He arrived at the USS *Carl Vinson* after a discussion with his detailer, a navy assignment counselor. Both agreed that being a public affairs officer was a challenging job offering many opportunities and rewards. The public affairs office of an aircraft carrier is the hub of a navy battle group's public relations program—and the battle group is often the first military force dispatched to any emergency or contingency worldwide. Since there are only thirteen aircraft carriers in the navy, only thirteen people navywide hold the job at any one time. "That is exciting in itself," Butts says.

Aboard the *Carl Vinson*, Butts had five journalists working for him to publish the ship's daily newspaper, operate the twenty-four-hour-a-day radio and TV stations, handle media inquiries and information requests from the public, and produce special training videos. Each journalist also had a second job on board, part of a locker damage-control team for general quarters, often called battle stations. In an emergency, they were also integrated into this team to fight fires, stop flooding, and save lives. "Whatever was happening, we had to be prepared to handle it," he says.

Marking Time. With essentially two jobs to work, the hours can get long. Barring any urgent work, Butts would usually turn in about 11 P.M., after sending the paper to press at 10 P.M. He would break up his schedule with a trip to the gym at 3 P.M.—the midpoint for his day. Being busy can be good in that it staves off the loneliness of being away from home. Important holidays come and go with sailors often unable to connect physically with their families. Instead they e-mail, write letters, and occasionally talk on the phone.

Even the travel loses a bit of luster. "Exploring foreign ports is great fun, but it is something I'd rather share with my family," Butts says. "It helps knowing that you are doing something for your country. You are deployed at the holidays so others can enjoy them in peace, safe from danger.

"My favorite part of my job is that it is always changing. I never get bored. My least favorite part is that it is always changing, so it's hard to develop a routine."

Advice from David Butts. Butts says that the men and women who join the navy represent a cross section of America and the best it has to offer. "Back in their hometowns, these young men and women are heroes. Their moms and dads and grandparents and brothers and sisters are all very proud of what our sailors do. To me, being around all of these heroes makes mine the best job in the world."

In addition, the navy gives you everything you need to thrive, including training and the chance to use it. "We have eighteen-year-old men and women steering this ninety-five-thousand-ton ship," Butts says. "I've seen eighteen-year-olds drive cars back home, and I wouldn't trust many of them with my life. But we teach them how; we stand by to catch them if they stumble; we give them full faith and confidence to do the job right; and we expect they will succeed. We are seldom disappointed."

In return, the navy expects your full commitment and energy. Navy life requires discipline and a sense of personal responsibility. It gives people an excellent opportunity to learn a skill, gain experience, and mature. It isn't for everyone. Butts advises talking to recruiters from different services and weighing your options. Decide what career you want to pursue, then see if the navy offers a program in that area.

CHAPTER THREE

Fishing for Money

C ommercial fishing harbors an air of romance akin to firefighting or detective work, and like those jobs, the romance
comes from those viewing it from the outside. Commercial
fishermen are subject to the same extended absences from family
as military sailors—trips may take weeks or even months, hundreds of miles from home port—but without the safety net of
military benefits and organization and with only seasonal work.
Fishermen often work independently with their own boats and
equipment; in fact, commercial fishing has one of the larger
independently employed workforces in North America. More
than 50 percent are self-employed.

But for an elite subset of hardy outdoors people, not fishing for
a living is not an option. It calls to them, and they know the sea
and the coasts as few others ever could. It also presents a chance
for enterprising types to earn a good living with a minimal
amount of formal education. (For information about merchant
marine occupations, see Chapter 4.)

The Work

Fishermen gather aquatic species for grocery distributors and for
use as animal feed, bait, and for other purposes. Fishing hundreds
of miles from shore with commercial vessels—large boats capable
of hauling a catch of tens of thousands of pounds of fish—
requires a crew that includes a captain, or skipper; a first mate;
sometimes a second mate, called a boatswain; and deckhands.

The pace of work varies—it's intense while netting and hauling the catch aboard and relatively relaxed while traveling between home port and the fishing grounds. However, lookout watches— usually six hours long—are a regular responsibility, and crew members must be prepared to stand watch at prearranged times of the day or night.

Although fishing gear has improved and operations have become more mechanized, netting and processing fish are exhausting activities. Even though newer vessels have improved living quarters and amenities such as television and shower stalls, crews still experience the aggravations of confined conditions, continuous close personal contact, and sea swells that constantly rock the boat.

The work entails strenuous outdoor labor and long hours under almost every kind of weather and sea conditions imaginable, depending on the species of fish the crew is seeking. Fishermen work under hazardous conditions, and often help is not readily available. Divers are affected by murky water and unexpected shifts in currents. Malfunctioning navigation or communication equipment may lead to collisions or even shipwrecks. Broken gear poses a danger to the crew, who must also guard against entanglement in fishing nets, decks made slippery by fish-processing operations, ice formation in the winter, and being swept overboard—a potentially fatal situation. Divers must beware of entangled air lines, malfunctioning scuba equipment, decompression problems, and attacks by predatory fish. Treatment for serious injuries may have to await transfer to a hospital. And danger from incapacitating injuries is especially high.

Diving and Shallow-Water Fishing

A very small proportion of commercial fishing is conducted as diving operations. Depending upon the water's depth, divers, wearing regulation diving suits with an umbilical (air line) or a scuba outfit and equipment, use spears to catch fish and nets and other equipment to gather shellfish, coral, sea urchins, abalone, and sponges.

In very shallow waters, fish are caught from small boats with outboard motors, from rowboats, or by wading. Fishers use a wide variety of hand-operated equipment—nets, tongs, rakes, hoes, hooks, and shovels—to gather fish and shellfish, catch amphibians and reptiles such as frogs and turtles, and harvest marine vegetation such as Irish moss and kelp.

Sport Fishing

Although most fishermen are involved with commercial fishing, some captains and deckhands are primarily employed in sport or recreational fishing. Typically a group of people charters a fishing vessel for a period ranging from several hours to several days. They want to pursue sport fishing, socializing, and relaxation, and they employ a captain and possibly several deckhands. (See the interview with charter skipper and sailing instructor Lee Woods in Chapter 7.)

The Crew

The size of the crew depends on the size of the boat and the operation itself. Smaller boats operate closer to shore and might have just a few on crew, working around bays and inlets. Larger boats tend to be more technologically advanced and are designed to fish in deep water, to remain at sea for much longer, and even to process the catch right there. Their crews usually have the following members.

Captain

The captain plans and oversees the fishing operation—the fish to be sought, the location of the best fishing grounds, the method of capture, the duration of the trip, and the sale of the catch. The captain ensures that the fishing vessel is in suitable condition;

oversees the purchase of supplies, gear, and equipment such as fuel, netting, and cables; and hires qualified crew members and assigns their duties. The vessel's course is plotted with navigation aids such as compasses, sextants, and charts; crew members use electronic equipment such as autopilots, a loran system, and satellites to navigate.

The ships also use radar to avoid obstacles and use depth sounders to indicate the water depth and the presence of marine life between the vessel and the seafloor. The captain directs the fishing operation through the officers and records daily activities in the ship's log. Upon returning to port, the captain arranges for the sale of the catch directly to buyers or through a fish auction and ensures that each crew member receives the prearranged portion of the adjusted net proceeds from the sale.

First Mate

The first mate, the captain's assistant, must be familiar with navigation requirements and the operation of all electronic equipment. The mate assumes control of the vessel when the captain is off duty. These duty shifts, called watches, usually last six hours. The mate's regular duty, with the help of the boatswain and under the captain's oversight, is to direct the fishing operations and sailing responsibilities of the deckhands. These include the operation, maintenance, and repair of the vessel and the gathering, preservation, stowing, and unloading of the catch.

Boatswain

The boatswain, a highly experienced deckhand with supervisory responsibilities, directs the deckhands as they carry out the sailing and fishing operations. Prior to departure, the boatswain directs the deckhands to load equipment and supplies, either manually or with hoisting equipment, and untie lines from other boats and the dock. When necessary, the boatswain repairs the fishing gear, equipment, nets, and accessories, operating the gear and letting out and pulling in nets and lines. The boatswain extracts the catch, such as pollock, flounder, menhaden, and tuna, from the nets or hooks.

Deckhand

Deckhands use dip nets to prevent the escape of small fish. They use gaffs, iron hooks with handles, to facilitate the landing of large fish. Then they wash, salt, ice, and stow the catch away. Deckhands also must ensure that decks are clear and clean at all times and that the vessel's engines and equipment are kept in good working order. Upon return to port, they secure the vessel's lines to and from the docks and other vessels. Unless lumpers, or laborers, are hired, the deckhands unload the catch.

Employment

Fishermen hold an estimated thirty-eight thousand jobs in the United States and forty-six thousand jobs in Canada, but don't forget that much of that work is part-time, so the number of jobs might fall by a quarter if calculated as full-time work. Opportunities are best in the summer and fall, when demand for these workers peaks.

Employment of fishermen is on the decline. Catch volume depends on the natural ability of stock to replenish itself through growth and reproduction. Many operations are at or beyond maximum sustainable yield, and the number of workers who can earn an adequate income from fishing is expected to decline. Most job openings will arise from the need to replace workers who retire or leave the occupation. Some fishermen leave the occupation because of the strenuous and hazardous nature of the job and the lack of steady, year-round income.

The use of sophisticated electronic equipment for navigation, communication, and locating fish has raised the efficiency of finding fish stocks. Also, improvements in fishing gear and the use of highly automated floating processors, where the catch is processed aboard the vessel, have greatly increased fish hauls. In many areas, particularly the North Atlantic and Pacific Northwest, damage to spawning grounds and excess fish harvesting capacity have adversely affected the stocks of fish and, consequently, the employment opportunities for fishermen. Some fisheries councils have issued various types of restrictions on harvesting to allow stocks of fish and shellfish to naturally replenish, thereby idling many fishers. In addition, low prices for some species and rising seafood imports are adversely affecting fishing income and also causing some fishers to leave the industry. Fishermen are also facing competition from the farmed-fish industry.

Governmental efforts to replenish stocks are having some positive results, which should increase the stock of fish in the future. Furthermore, efforts by private fishermen's associations on the West Coast to increase government monitoring of the fisheries may help to prevent the type of decline in fish stocks found in waters off the East Coast. Nevertheless, fewer fishermen and fishing vessel operators are expected to make their living on the open water in the years ahead.

There is, however, steady interest in recreational fishing, and though it's a much smaller market, some commercial fishermen could find work on sport fishing boats.

Getting Started

Fishermen generally acquire their skills on the job, many as members of families involved in fishing. No formal academic requirements exist. Job seekers can expedite entrance into fishing by enrolling in two-year vocational-technical programs offered by secondary schools, primarily in coastal areas. In addition, the University of Rhode Island offers a bachelor's degree program in aquaculture and fisheries technology (www.uri.edu/cels/acaddept/aqfishtech.html#) that includes courses in seamanship, vessel operations, marine safety, navigation, vessel repair and maintenance, health emergencies, and fishing gear technology and is accompanied by hands-on experience.

Experienced fishermen may find short-term workshops offered through various postsecondary institutions especially useful. These programs provide a good working knowledge of electronic equipment used in navigation and communication and the latest improvements in fishing gear.

Fishermen must be in good health and possess physical strength. Coordination and mechanical aptitude are necessary to operate, maintain, and repair equipment and fishing gear. On larger vessels, they must be able to work as members of a team. They must be patient yet alert to overcome the boredom of long watches when not engaged in fishing operations. The ability to assume any deckhand's functions on short notice is important. Mates must have supervisory ability and be able to assume either a deckhand's or the captain's duties when necessary. The captain must be highly experienced, mature, and decisive and have good business skills. Captains with initiative and the required capital often become boat owners.

On fishing vessels, most fishermen begin as deckhands. Deckhands whose experience and interests are in ship engineering— maintenance and repair of ship engines and equipment—can eventually become licensed chief engineers on large commercial vessels.

Divers in fishing operations can enter commercial diving—for example, doing ship repair and pier and marina maintenance— usually after completion of a certified training program sponsored by an educational institution or industry association. (See www.trade-schools.net/directory/diving-schools-directory.asp for a list of schools specializing in commercial diving.) Experienced, reliable deckhands who display supervisory qualities may become boatswains. Boatswains may, in turn, become first mates and, eventually, captains.

The overwhelming majority of captains eventually own or have an interest in one or more fishing boats. Some may choose to run a recreational or sport fishing operation. When their seagoing days are over, experienced individuals may work in stores selling fishing and marine equipment and supplies or, with the necessary capital, they might own one. Some captains may assume advisory or administrative positions in industry trade associations or government offices, such as harbor development commissions, or teaching positions in industry-sponsored workshops or in educational institutions.

Income

Full-time and salaried commercial fishermen earn between $320 and $775 a week, but income depends a lot on the size and type of boat, the type of catch, and the frequency of work. Money is best in the spring and fall, when fisheries are the busiest, and lowest during the winter. Many full-time and most part-time workers supplement their incomes by working in other jobs during the off-season. For example, fishers may work in seafood-processing plants, establishments selling fishing and marine equipment, or in construction.

The costs of the fishing operation—operating the ship, repair and maintenance of gear and equipment, and the crew's supplies—are deducted from the sale of the catch. The net proceeds are then distributed among the crew members in accordance with a prearranged percentage. Generally, the ship's owner, usually its captain, receives half of the net proceeds, which covers any profit as well as the depreciation, maintenance, and replacement costs of the ship.

CHAPTER FOUR

Civilian Sailors

Workers in water transportation occupations operate and maintain deep-sea merchant ships, tugboats, towboats, ferries, dredges, research vessels, and other waterborne craft on the oceans and the Great Lakes, in harbors, on rivers and canals, and on other waterways.

Captains or masters are in overall command of the operation of a vessel, and they supervise the work of the other officers and the crew. They set course and speed, maneuver the vessel to avoid hazards and other ships, and periodically determine position using navigation aids, celestial observations, and charts. They direct crew members to steer the vessel, operate engines, signal to other vessels, perform maintenance, and handle lines (operate docking, towing, or dredging gear). Captains ensure that proper procedures and safety practices are followed, check that machinery and equipment are in good working order, and oversee the loading and unloading of cargo or passengers. They also maintain logs and other records of the ships' movements and of the cargo carried.

Captains on large vessels are assisted by deck officers or mates. Merchant marine vessels—those carrying cargo overseas—have a chief or first mate, a second mate, and a third mate. Mates oversee the operation of the vessel or stand watch for specified periods, usually four hours on and eight hours off. On smaller vessels, there may be only one mate, called a pilot on some inland vessels, who alternates watches with the captain.

Engineers or marine engineers operate, maintain, and repair propulsion engines, boilers, generators, pumps, and other machinery. Merchant marine vessels usually have four engineering officers: a chief engineer and a first, second, and third assistant engineer. Assistant engineers stand periodic watches, overseeing the operation of engines and machinery.

Deckhands, particularly on inland waters, operate the vessel and its deck equipment under the direction of the ship's officers and keep the nonengineering areas in good condition. They stand watch, looking out for other vessels, obstructions in the ship's path, and aids to navigation. They also steer the ship, measure water depth in shallow areas, and maintain and operate deck equipment such as lifeboats, anchors, and cargo-handling gear. When docking or departing, they handle lines. They also perform maintenance chores such as repairing lines, chipping rust, and painting and cleaning decks and other areas. Deckhands may also load and unload cargo. On vessels handling liquid cargo, they hook up hoses, operate pumps, and clean tanks. Deckhands on tugboats or tow vessels tie barges together into tow units, inspect them periodically, and disconnect them when the destination is reached. Larger vessels have a boatswain or head deckhand.

Marine oilers work below decks under the direction of the ship's engineers. They lubricate the gears, shafts, bearings, and other moving parts of engines and motors, read pressure and temperature gauges and record data, and may repair and adjust machinery.

A typical deep-sea merchant ship has a captain, three deck officers or mates, a chief engineer and three assistant engineers, plus six or more deckhands and oilers. Depending on their size, vessels operating in harbors, rivers, or along the coast may have a crew comprising only a captain and one deckhand, or they may have a captain, mate or pilot, engineer, and as many as seven or eight deckhands. Large vessels also have a full-time cook and helper, while on small ones a deckhand does the cooking. Merchant ships also have an electrician, machinery mechanics, and a radio officer.

Pilots guide ships in and out of harbors, through straits, and on rivers and other confined waterways where a familiarity with local water depths, winds, tides, currents, and hazards such as reefs and shoals is of prime importance. Pilots on river and canal vessels usually are regular crew members, like mates. Harbor pilots are generally independent contractors who accompany vessels while they enter or leave port. They may pilot many ships in a single day.

Merchant mariners are away from home for extended periods but earn long leaves. Most are hired for one voyage, with no job security after that. At sea, they usually stand watch for four hours and are off for eight hours, seven days a week. Those employed on Great Lakes ships work sixty days and have thirty days off but do not often work in the winter. Workers on rivers and canals and in harbors are more likely to have year-round work. Some work eight- or twelve-hour shifts and go home every day. Others work steadily for a week or month and then have an extended period off. When working, they are usually on duty for six or twelve hours and are off for six or twelve hours.

People in water transportation occupations work in all kinds of weather conditions, and, although merchant mariners try to avoid severe storms while at sea, working in damp and cold conditions is unpleasant. It is uncommon for vessels to sink, but workers nevertheless face the possibility that they may have to abandon their craft on short notice if it collides with other vessels or runs aground. They also risk injury or death from falling overboard and hazards associated with working with machinery, heavy loads, and dangerous cargo.

Some newer vessels are air-conditioned, soundproofed from noisy machinery, and have comfortable living quarters. However, some workers do not like the long periods away from home and the confinement aboard ship.

Getting Started

Entry, training, and educational requirements for most water transportation occupations are established and regulated by the U.S. Coast Guard and the marine arm of Transport Canada. All officers and operators of watercraft must be licensed by the U.S. Coast Guard or Transport Canada. Licensing differs somewhat between the merchant marine and others.

Deck and engineering officers in the merchant marine must be licensed. For details on qualifying for a license, see www.uscg .mil/stcw in the United States and www.tc.gc.ca/marinesafety/ mpsp/menu.htm in Canada. A physical examination and a drug test are required to gain a license. In general, people with at least three years of appropriate sea experience can be licensed if they pass the written exam, but it is difficult to pass without substantial formal schooling or independent study. Also, because sailors may work six months a year or less, it can take five to eight years to accumulate the necessary experience.

Employment in the merchant marine as an unlicensed sailor requires some official paperwork known as a Merchant Mariner's Document (MMD). Applicants for the MMD do not need to be U.S. citizens, or Canadian citizens in Canada, so long as they can prove their status as lawful permanent residents. A medical certificate of excellent health and a certificate attesting to vision, color perception, and general physical condition may be required for higher-level deckhands. While no experience or formal schooling is required, training at a union-operated school is helpful. Beginners are classified as ordinary deckhands and may be assigned to the deck or engineering department. With experience at sea, and perhaps union-sponsored training, an ordinary deckhand can pass the able seaman exam. Merchant marine officers and deckhands, both experienced and beginner, are hired for voyages through union hiring halls or directly by shipping companies.

Harbor pilot training is usually an apprenticeship with a shipping company or a pilot employees association. Entrants may be able seamen or licensed officers.

No training or experience is needed to become a seaman or deckhand on vessels operating in harbors or on rivers or other waterways. Newly hired workers generally learn skills on the job. With experience, they could qualify to become mates, pilots, or captains. Substantial knowledge gained through experience, courses in seamanship schools, and independent study are needed to pass those exams.

Employment

Water transportation workers hold more than seventy-two thousand jobs, but the total number who worked at some point in the year was probably twice that because many merchant marine officers and seamen work only part of the year. In Canada the figure is around twenty-eight thousand.

In the United States about 33 percent of water transportation workers were employed aboard ship—about 17 percent working in inland water transportation—primarily the Mississippi River system—with the other 16 percent employed in water transportation on the deep seas, along the coasts, and on the Great Lakes. Another 25 percent worked in establishments related to port and harbor operations, marine cargo handling, or navigational services to shipping. The federal government employed approximately 5 percent of all water transportation workers, most of whom worked on supply ships and are civilian mariners of the navy's Military Sealift Command. The remaining water transportation workers were employed on vessels carrying passengers, such as cruise ships, casino boats, sightseeing and excursion boats, and ferries.

Keen competition is expected to continue for jobs in water transportation. Overall, employment in water transportation is projected to decline through 2014. Employment in deep-sea shipping is expected to stabilize after several years of decline. International regulations have raised shipping standards with respect to safety, training, and working conditions. Consequently, competition from ships that sail under foreign "flags of convenience" (flags of countries whose employment base and regulations are economically favorable to shipowners) has lessened as the standards of operation have become more uniform. This has made the costs of operating U.S. and Canadian ships more comparable to foreign-flagged ships and has modestly increased the amount of international cargo they carry. For the United States, a fleet of deep-sea ships is also considered to be vital to defense, so some receive federal support through a maritime security subsidy and other legal provisions that limit certain federal cargo to ships flying the U.S. flag.

Moderating the growth in water transportation occupations is a projected decline in the number of vessels operating on the Great Lakes and inland waterways. Vessels on rivers and canals and on the Great Lakes carry mostly bulk products, such as coal, iron ore, petroleum, sand and gravel, grain, and chemicals. Although shipments of most of these products are expected to grow for several years, steel imports are dampening employment on the Great Lakes.

Job openings will also result from the need to replace those leaving the occupation. Some experienced merchant mariners may continue to go without work for varying periods. However, this situation appears to be changing, with demand for licensed and unlicensed personnel rising. Maritime academy graduates who have not found licensed shipboard jobs in the U.S. merchant marine could find jobs in related industries. Some take land-based jobs with shipping companies, marine insurance companies, manufacturers of boilers or related machinery, or other related jobs.

Earnings

Earnings vary widely with the particular water transportation position and the worker's experience, ranging from the minimum wage for some beginning seamen or mate positions to more than $42 per hour in 2004 for some experienced ship engineers. Ship engineers earned a median wage of $26.42 per hour; captains and mates, $24.20; motorboat operators, $15.39; and sailors and marine oilers, $14.

Annual pay for captains of larger vessels, such as container ships, oil tankers, or passenger ships, may reach six figures even in the United States, but only after many years of experience. Similarly, captains of tugboats often earn more than the median, with earnings dependent on the port and the nature of the cargo.

What It's Really Like

Find out what it takes to be a civilian sailor and whether you share the passion of Thomas MacPherson, a longtime shipboard engineer.

Thomas MacPherson, Chief Engineer

Thomas MacPherson came to his present job as chief engineer on an elevator support ship from a navy family. Both his father and older brother were in the U.S. Navy, and he spent eighteen years there as well before taking early retirement. He had fourteen years of sea time with the U.S. Navy and one year with Edison Chouest Offshore, an offshore support enterprise that is based in Galiano, Louisiana.

"I chose joining the navy to leave the area where I grew up (McKeesport, Pennsylvania) because the steel industry was dying out and I wanted to see something different," MacPherson says. His new postretirement job is similar to what he did in the navy, although it's less intense and more informal—"and a lot more fun," he adds. As a chief engineer, he supervises and operates the engine room and other mechanical aspects of the ship for a company that transports crews and supplies to and from oil rigs. It also transports "liquid mud"—fill material pumped into oil wells to force out the oil. The company does a lot of work with various U.S. Navy projects, such as submarine testing and even the recovery of major equipment lost at sea.

Approaching the Job. MacPherson's job requires keeping maintenance logs, checking fuel and water levels, and monitoring and repairing engine components and electrical equipment, his favorite part of the job. He says he enjoys the day-to-day variety of his work and learns something new every day. He might operate the boat's diesel engines, work on the phone lines, help the deckhands with the odd task, or operate the hydraulic system to lower the submarine elevator system, for example. "As long as they are done safely and correctly, there are very few things you can't do," he says.

Like others who spend a lot of time at sea, MacPherson laments the separation from family, but he says he does enjoy getting away now and again and the chance to catch up on reading or watch a movie. The job pays well and provides food and a bunk.

Advice from Thomas MacPherson. MacPherson says a lot of junior engineers start out as ordinary seamen or in seagoing services such as the navy, as he did. Any time put in on a boat is good experience, whether it's on a container ship in the Gulf of Mexico, a tanker in Alaska, or a fishing rig on the northern Atlantic Coast. "Sea time is sea time," he says. Captains do look for some seagoing experience before hiring.

In MacPherson's case, knowledge of diesels is a prerequisite for engineers on the offshore vessel he works on. For ocean vessels, steam and/or diesel knowledge would be necessary, and in both cases, electrical and fluid system knowledge would be required. It's possible to shorten some requirements by attending one of the merchant marine academies, but U.S. Navy or U.S. Coast Guard sea time is partially credited toward merchant marine sea time. See www.usmm.org/links.html (click on "Maritime Academies" near the top of the page) or www.hal-pc.org/~nugent/school.html for links to maritime academies. Just as important as credentials, however, are dependability, responsibility, and patience. And most important, MacPherson says, "You shouldn't be afraid of hard work."

CHAPTER FIVE

Cruising the Open Water

To work aboard a cruise ship is to work at the junction of two worlds. In one sense, life for the crew of a cruise ship is not unlike serving on staff as part of any seagoing experience. There are regulations and protocol to follow, the majesty and isolation of being at sea for long periods of time, the thrill of travel to faraway lands, and the burden of being on call in some fashion twenty-four hours a day. But for cruise staff, there's also the world of hospitality. Jobs must not only get done, but get done with a smile that encourages guests to come back. Meeting their needs is a top priority. Above all, guests must have fun, which, happily for staff, means bright, cheerful surroundings, appealing weather and destinations, and entertainment options aplenty.

The destinations and areas of operation are more diverse than you might expect. Probably the best-known and among the most popular are midlength getaway vacation cruises operating out of ports in southern Florida and sailing to Mexico, the Bahamas, Puerto Rico, the Dominican Republic, and other Caribbean islands. Another popular route is on the West Coast from Southern California to the Mexican Riviera. Often, because of the economic advantage, these cruise ships fly "flags of convenience," meaning they operate under the auspices of some other country favorable to their interests but serve primarily a clientele from the United States and Canada. This is changing, however. In the wake of September 11, the United States has recognized the value of having commercial U.S.–flagged ships available in its fleet should it need to call on those resources during armed conflicts, and the government has passed legislation motivating cruise lines to bring a few ships back under the U.S. flag.

Less top-of-mind are the ships and boats operating up and down the Atlantic and Pacific coasts. These tend to operate in opposite fashions, the Atlantic lines carrying passengers from the Northeast to warm Southern destinations, and the Pacific lines running from ports in the Pacific Northwest, such as Vancouver and Seattle, to Alaska. Other lines ply South America, the Mediterranean, transatlantic routes to Europe, the Hawaiian Islands, the Mississippi River basin, and the Great Lakes. Also popular in Florida, Massachusetts, New York, and South Carolina are "cruises to nowhere" that travel beyond state lines to permit legal gambling aboard ship.

Cruises have grown exponentially more popular in recent years and are now among the fastest-growing businesses anywhere. Between 2000 and 2006, cruise lines launched seventy-four major new ships, and another thirty-two are scheduled for delivery by 2010, meaning tens of thousands of new jobs. Not only are there more cruises and cruise ships, but companies are battling each other to market the biggest and most luxurious ships. Now dozens of ships can carry more than 100,000 tons, a size unknown until the late 1990s, and the 200,000-ton cruise ship is on the horizon. Royal Caribbean's Genesis class of cruise ships, for example, forthcoming in 2009, should set size records at 220,000 gross tons. (The *Titanic*, by comparison, had a gross tonnage of 46,000.)

Cruise Ship Staffing

Cruise lines employ all sorts of personnel to handle the many tasks involved with running a ship. A small ship with 850 passengers might have more than 600 crew members; larger ships with 2,500 or so passengers could employ 1,500 or more crew members.

As the size of the industry, the size of the ships, and the number of amenities aboard have grown, staff sizes have increased as well, and it's not unheard of for staff to outnumber passengers on high-end ships.

Service Jobs

The marine crew—the captain, deckhands, deck officers, oilers, and engineering officers—generally come from the ship's point of origin—Greece, Norway, or Italy, for example—so most of the jobs open to Americans are found within hotel operations, the guest administration aspect of the operation.

To fully understand what a cruise is like, think of it as a floating hotel and amusement park rolled into one. Just as these places have different personalities and amenities, so do cruises. Some ships are extremely luxurious, offering five-star food and service. Others cater to a younger, more casual crowd.

Whatever style the cruise, most employ crews to work in the following positions:

Accountant
Assistant Cruise Director
Beautician
Casino Operator
Cruise Director
Cruise Staff/Activities
DJ
Doctor
Entertainer
Gift Shop Manager/Assistant
Nurse
Port Lecturer
Photographer
Purser
Reservationist

Sales Manager
Shore Excursions Director
Sports/Fitness Director
Steward
Waiter
Youth Counselor

Job titles and responsibilities vary from ship to ship. For example, the term *cruise staff* might be synonymous with *assistant cruise director* or *activities director*.

Cruise Staff on the Clock

Although filled with their share of excitement and glamour, cruise ship jobs involve a lot of hard work. Cruise staffs put in long hours—anywhere from eight to fifteen hours a day, seven days a week when under way—and must maintain a high level of energy and always be cordial and friendly to passengers.

Cruise staff members are generally involved with organizing activities and social events, including common shipboard games such as shuffleboard and ring toss, bingo, aerobics classes, basketball, golf putting (and driving—off the stern of the ship), and pool games. They also participate in cocktail parties and masquerade balls and take every opportunity to make sure passengers feel comfortable and enjoy themselves. Many of the cruise staff also double as entertainers and have some talent for performing, whether as singers, musicians, or DJs.

When in port, most of the crew members are allowed to go ashore and have time off to explore, although some function as chaperones, helping passengers find their way around foreign locales or recommending certain shops or restaurants to disembarking passengers. Much of the security staff must remain behind to keep watch aboard the ship.

Activities usually follow a rigid schedule, with little time in between for the crew to rest or take a break. With a constant eye on their watches, cruise staffs run from one activity to another, announcing games over the loudspeaker, setting up the deck for exercise classes, supervising games or other special events, and encouraging everyone to participate. An outgoing, energetic individual would be in his or her element in such a job.

Earnings

While salaries are not overly generous, cruise jobs do have certain benefits. For two things, staff members receive free housing and all the food they can eat while on board the ship. A full-time employee doesn't need to reserve money for an apartment or house, and since purchasing options are rather limited on the ship, it's possible to save quite a bit of money. Often companies pay transportation costs to get you to port when you start. Cruise ships also sail to exotic ports, giving staff members the chance to travel and meet people from all over the world.

Annual salaries don't mean much, since cruise seasons vary depending on the locale and staff often don't work year-round. Still, a chief purser could earn $4,300 to $5,800 per month, and a junior assistant purser $1,600 to $1,800 per month. A cruise director might expect to earn $3,800 to $7,500 per month, an assistant cruise director $2,100 to $2,700 per month, and cruise staff $1,800 to $2,100 per month. Assistant cruise directors and other cruise staff can move up the ladder to more supervisory and managerial positions. They need to demonstrate that they have organizational skills and that they can delegate and manage people. They also must be good at detail work and paperwork. Sometimes earning a promotion has to do with how much experience you have and how good you are—or with who has quit or otherwise moved on.

Getting Started

A college education is not necessary to work on a cruise line, but some prefer to see an applicant with a degree in psychology, hotel management, physical education, or communications. It's also a good idea to know another language, especially Spanish or German. Even more important are the personal qualities a good cruise staff member should possess: patience, diplomacy, energy, enthusiasm, and athleticism or artistry. Most successful applicants land their jobs by applying directly to the various cruise lines, which are located mainly in South Florida, Los Angeles, New York, and Seattle. For a list of cruise lines and other resources, please see the Appendix.

What It's Really Like

Cruise jobs are not all the same. Whether you'd love it depends on matching your personality and talents to the proper position. Chief Purser Richard Turnwald and assistant cruise director Beverly Citron describe their very different jobs in these profiles.

Richard Turnwald, Cruise Ship Purser

Richard Turnwald has worked in the cruise industry for more than fourteen years. He started out shoreside in the operations department, where he handled everything from personnel to ordering supplies for the ships. He went on to positions with the cruise staff as a shore excursions director, assistant cruise director, and port lecturer, providing information on the different ports of call. He then worked his way up from junior purser to chief purser.

"Ever since I was a little boy, I've always loved ships and the sea," he says. "I read about them and studied them, and there was no doubt in my mind that I wanted to be involved in some way with ships as a profession."

While in college in Michigan, he began sending out his resume to cruise lines, most of which were based in Miami. After a phone interview, he took a job with the office administration. "That was exciting and scary at the same time," he says. "I was just out of college, and I had to relocate to a place where I didn't know anyone, but it was like a dream for me to finally be able to work closely with the cruise ships."

Minding the Store. Turnwald quickly adapted to the purser's office and overall cruise ship environment. Aside from being on the ship, it isn't all that different from working at the front desk of a big hotel. The staff members handle all the money on the ship, pay all the bills and the salaries, cash traveler's checks for passengers, provide safes for valuables, fill out all the documentation for customs and immigration officials in the different countries, and perform other crucial behind-the-scenes functions. The purser is who passengers come to for information or help with problems. He's in charge of cabin assignments and also coordinates with medical personnel to help handle any emergencies.

As chief purser, Turnwald is responsible for the entire financial aspect of the ship's operation and oversees a staff of six, although larger ships could have fifteen people or more. There are ascending ranks for pursers: junior or assistant purser, second purser, first purser, then chief purser. Promotions are based on ability—how well you do your job—as well as the length of time you've been employed. "I was fortunate," Turnwald says. "I rose up through the ranks fairly quickly. Within three months I'd worked my way up from junior purser to chief purser. But that's really an exceptional situation. It usually takes a good year or so. It depends on how many people are ahead of you, if they leave or stay."

Shipboard Life. Turnwald emphasizes that prospective employees can't go in expecting the same experience on staff as they would as a guest. The living conditions are much more modest. You might share a room with one or two other employees, and the food is a grade or two below what the passengers are eating upstairs as well. "They might be having lobster and steak," he says, "but the crew is eating fish or meat loaf."

While living aboard a ship might sound appealing, keep in mind you also live your job—you're on duty seven days a week, and you might not have a day off for several months at a time. On the positive side, there's no commute to work, your housing is free, and you get several hours off at a time when the ship is in port.

"I've been all over the world, to places I wouldn't have had the time or money to get to otherwise," Turnwald says. "I've been to the Caribbean, Alaska, South America, Antarctica, Europe, Hawaii. If you're on an itinerary that repeats every week, you get to know that place very well and the people there, so that's a plus.

"And there's something so relaxing and peaceful about being at sea—just to stand by the railing of the deck and see the changes in the weather and the whales and the other sea life. Another advantage is the money. You work hard and very intensely for long periods of time, but typically you're paid well, and it's a good opportunity to save money. I was able to buy a house."

Advice from Richard Turnwald. Work on people skills, and try to be friendly, helpful, and courteous at all times. "It's very important," he says. "You'll be representing the cruise line to a lot of people. And you have to be willing and able to accept orders. It isn't as strict as the navy, but when you're on a ship, there are a lot of rules and guidelines you have to follow." If you're too independent-minded and prefer to roam according to your own schedule, ship life probably isn't for you.

Beverley Citron, Assistant Cruise Director

Beverley Citron began working on cruise ships at age twenty-one as a hairdresser. Realizing she would enjoy being part of a staff with more interaction, she took time off to study singing and guitar and put together an act with musical arrangements and costumes. "I was determined to get a job as a social staff member," she says. Her hard work paid off, and she landed her first job as a youth counselor planning activities at a sailing club in England.

"After all those years of applying, when I got that letter in the mail saying 'Beverley, we have selected you to be a youth counselor. . . . We'll be sending you an air ticket. . . . Please get your visa sorted out,' I was literally speechless," she says. "That was probably the happiest moment of my life."

She has since also worked as a social director for a resort, a sports director, and an assistant cruise director.

Welcome to the Social. The cruise staff members are in charge of all the games, activities, and shore excursions for the passengers, similar to being a camp counselor but for adults. They make sure the passengers are having fun and try to come up with activities and events to capture their interest. "We might organize a grandmother's tea or give an origami (paper folding) demonstration or stage a treasure hunt," Citron says. "When in port, we might chaperone a group of passengers on a tour. Even between scheduled activities, we constantly interact and socialize with the passengers."

The team quickly becomes a de facto family. Some share cabins at night and work closely during the day. Citron dismisses the idea that the staff suffers claustrophobia or a sea-bound form of cabin fever. Most staff members have the chance to go ashore when the ship's in port, and they can shop, dance in nightclubs, go to the beach, or do anything else that's within reach.

The freedom of port counterbalances the occasional grind of being at sea. There are no days off when the ship is under way. "You have to be constantly energetic and cheerful, even when you don't feel like it," Citron says. "You could work up to fifteen hours a day, but what else are you going to do? The alternative is sitting in your cabin."

Her least favorite aspect is clock-watching. Social activities are heavily scheduled, and as an assistant cruise director, she has to make sure things run on time. "You have to be on the sports deck by nine, down in the lounge by nine-thirty, getting ready in your cabin to be back up on the deck by ten, and so on," she says.

Still, she calls working on a cruise ship her dream job and looks forward to it every morning. "I'm not an office person; it's very difficult for me to stay at a desk all day," she says. "I've got a lot of energy, and it's great for me being able to move about the ship making lots of friends, being busy."

Advice from Beverley Citron. Citron says many people give up too easily. She sent her resume to thirty-six cruise lines every three months, and it took her a few years to get in. But eventually it paid off. With the market for cruises growing so fast, today's newbies should have a much easier time. Cruise lines are hiring all the time. It's just a matter of deciding where you want to go and what you want to do. And, of course, having some prior experience will help fatten your paycheck.

CHAPTER SIX

Aquatic Heroes

O ur oceans, lakes, rivers, canals, ponds, and swimming pools are magnets for people who enjoy water sports and recreation. But where there's water, there's also a need for caution—and, more often than not, water rescue. About 70 percent of all boating fatalities are from drowning, and more than 90 percent of the victims were not wearing life vests. Alcohol is involved in one-third of fatal accidents.

Aquatic types who want to mitigate these statistics have an abundance of opportunities to consider. The idea of lifeguarding immediately leaps to mind, though that position might well be a stepping-stone to any number of water safety careers: firefighter, police officer, park ranger or warden, paramedic or emergency medical technician (EMT), diver, or work in the navy or coast guard. (See Chapter 2 for details on these last two occupations.) Each presents its own rewards and challenges and physically rigorous regimens that keep you alert and engaged. In addition, several positions, such as swim instructor, swim coach, and boating instructor, require safety skills as part of the job. Find out more about these positions in Chapter 7.

If you do have strong swim skills and the desire to train and commit to this type of work, you can find employment in a variety of settings. A select list includes:

Apartments
City and county parks and recreation departments
Community centers

Cruise ships
Day and overnight camps
Health and athletic clubs
National parks
Private country and yacht clubs
Red Cross facilities
Resorts
Water parks
YMCA/YWCAs

The type of training you'll need depends largely upon the setting in which you prefer to work. A camp or recreation center lifeguard will need to learn basic CPR and lifesaving techniques. (See www.redcross.org or www.redcross.ca to find professional Red Cross lifesaving training programs in your area.) A firefighter, a paramedic, a national park ranger, or a rescue diver will have a much more intensive training program and will be able to respond to a variety of rescue situations. Specialized training will depend on your area of responsibility. Of the settings listed above, we will examine three employers of water safety and rescue personnel in detail: camps, the national parks, and fire and rescue departments.

Camps

Approximately 75 percent of summer camps, both resident and day camps, are sponsored or run by social service agencies and nonprofit groups such as religious organizations, the YMCA or YWCA, Boy Scouts, Girl Scouts, Scouts Canada, or Girl Guides of Canada. Others are operated by school systems or are privately owned.

Camps can be day or resident. Trip camping offers programs in which groups move from site to site, whether by their own power or by vehicle or animal.

Each summer approximately half a million jobs are filled by high school and college students, teachers, doctors, nurses, food service staff and directors, sports specialists, and waterfront instructors and safety professionals. Most camps begin their summer seasons in late May or June and run until the middle or end of August. Few camps are open after Labor Day.

Aquatic Staff

Whether situated lakeside or by a pool or even at the ocean, most day and resident camps prominently feature waterfront activities, including swim instruction, water safety, and sometimes boating as a cornerstone of their summer programs.

While many specialty camp jobs do not require specific certification, waterfront jobs usually do. Although waterfront activities can often offer the most pleasure—what could be nicer than jumping into a refreshing spring-fed lake to cool off during a hot summer day?—they can also present the most danger. Waterfront staff must be skilled, observant supervisors and well versed in safety procedures and lifesaving and rescue techniques, as well as first aid. Information on finding jobs in camps is provided in Chapter 7.

Camps seeking to hire swimming and boating instructors and lifeguards often expect their staff members to show proof of professional training and generally want them to possess Red Cross certification.

American Red Cross Courses. Here is a sampling of courses offered by the American Red Cross that lead to certification:

LIFEGUARD CERTIFICATION COURSE
- **Purpose:** Teach lifeguards the skills and knowledge needed to prevent and respond to aquatic emergencies.
- **Includes:** Adult, child, and infant cardiopulmonary resuscitation (CPR); CPR for the professional rescuer; and first aid

certification. Must be fifteen years of age and attend every session.

- **Learning objectives:** Learn how to understand the value of behaving in a professional manner. Learn how to recognize the characteristic behaviors of distressed swimmers, as well as active and passive drowning victims. Learn to recognize an aquatic emergency and act promptly and appropriately. Learn equipment-based rescue skills and techniques used by professional lifeguards. Learn how to recognize and care for a possible spinal injury. Learn how to provide first aid and CPR. Course options include Lifeguarding (traditional), Waterfront Lifeguarding, Waterpark Lifeguarding, and Shallow Water Attendant.

- **Prerequisites:** Must be able to swim five hundred yards— one hundred yards each of the front crawl, breaststroke, and sidestroke (the remaining two hundred yards are the participant's choice); tread water for two minutes using legs only, crossing arms across the chest; submerge to a minimum depth of seven feet, retrieve a ten-pound object, and return it to the surface.

- **Certification requirements:** Successfully complete two written exams with a minimum score of 80 percent; complete two final rescue scenarios; perform all critical skills.

- **Course length:** Lengths vary from thirty to thirty-seven hours.

- **Certificate validity:** Lifeguard Training (including first aid), three years; CPR for the Professional Rescuer, one year.

SPORTS SAFETY TRAINING

- **Purpose:** Provide training in aquatic safety for coaches, athletic trainers, and others interested in sports to help coaches prevent and respond to sports-related injuries.
- **Prerequisites:** None.
- **Learning objectives:** Learn to identify and eliminate potentially hazardous conditions in various sports environments,

recognize emergencies, and make appropriate decisions for first aid care. Learn CPR and first aid treatment.

* **Course length:** Suggested minimum is eight hours.
* **Certification requirements:** Successfully complete final skills test and pass written test with a minimum score of 80 percent.
* **Certificate validity:** Three years.

What It's Really Like

Working at a summer camp can have many of the same benefits as attending one—making new friends, learning new skills, and being outside all day. But on staff, you also get to be the authority figure that dozens of kids look up to every day.

Rose Elizabeth Ledbetter, Lifeguard

As a student at Jacksonville State University in Alabama working toward a B.A. in English, Rose Elizabeth Ledbetter worked for two years as a camp lifeguard.

The Morning Routine. Ledbetter's experience seems typical for a young lifeguard. At camp, the approach was casual. Ledbetter and the other lifeguards would skip breakfast and sleep until about 8:45, then slip down to the waterfront in a hat and swimsuit ten minutes before the kids arrived. "The chlorine had to be tested first thing in the morning, but that only took one person," Ledbetter says. "One of us got up at 6:30, threw on a suit, tested the levels, and added chlorine. The rest of us slept in."

The usual lifeguard look was a tank with a sports bra underneath, a baseball cap with hair sticking out the back, and a pair of oversize men's boxer shorts with the waist rolled down. "The one must was a hat," she says. "Even those of us with the darkest complexions needed a hat. I'd always thought my fair skin didn't tan, but even with layers of sunscreen, after a few monster burns I got the tan of a lifetime."

Everyone in the Pool. At the beginning of the season, lifeguards would have campers form a single-file line at the gate and direct them to walk in quietly and sit at the edge of the pool. They'd explain the rules of the pool: no horseplay, no running, no diving in the shallow end, no hanging on the rope, no pushing, no hanging on the lifeguard chair. The foundation of pool safety at camp was the buddy system: every camper pairs up with another person of the same ability and sticks close to him or her whenever in the water. For odd-numbered groups, three campers could team up. Then, during regular swims, lifeguards would whistle occasionally and ask buddies to clasp hands to make sure everyone was accounted for.

In order to gauge ability, lifeguards administered a swim test to campers on the first day. The test was to swim the length of the pool on the deep side of the rope. "That was pretty funny," Ledbetter says. "You wouldn't believe the kids who lied about their swimming abilities to stay with their friends. We also made the counselors take the test after one too many adults lied about their abilities as well."

The Moment of Truth. Aside from swim-test tricks, Ledbetter soon found that much of lifeguarding is a struggle to stay alert and responsive when very little is happening. "We just sat there looking cool in our shades, swinging our whistles off the ends of our fingers, and watching the campers swim," she says. "On 'Baywatch,' they used to save three or four people on every show, but the truth was not nearly so exciting." Instead there might be one or two incidents per week combined, mostly with swimmers who overestimated their ability and panicked while in difficult situations.

Ledbetter's first true rescue came with an adult chaperone who had a heart attack in the pool. She reacted quickly and was able to get him out of the water and administer CPR, but even then reality didn't correspond to television drama. "In all of the lifeguarding classes and the CPR classes I'd taken, no one had informed me that a drowning victim could throw up in your mouth," she says. She managed to cope and stayed calm until the ambulance had left, but then she walked out to a nearby clump of bushes and got sick herself.

Clean-up Duty. When things were slow, the lifeguards were also tasked with cleaning the nearly Olympic-size pool and its ten-foot deep end. In a rigged fashion, they would balance atop an aluminum folding chair resting on the bottom of the pool, which barely allowed them to keep their heads above water, and use a long-handled brush to scrub the bottom. The sides could be cleaned from outside the pool. Ledbetter doesn't rank it among her favorite aspects of the job. "A person can get hypothermia even in eighty-degree water in less than an hour," she says. "So we were careful to work in short shifts. The work was exhausting and freezing."

Advice from Rose Elizabeth Ledbetter. Ledbetter advises getting your certification—and getting in shape—before the start of summer. Once the season begins and camp directors are eager to bring staff on board, you won't have time. Most certification programs require that you be at least sixteen to obtain a license. In some cases, the minimum age is eighteen. Check with your state or province to find out. The American Red Cross and the YMCA (or Canadian Red Cross and YMCA Canada) are the main certifying bodies.

Among other tasks, you will be required to know how to do the breaststroke, backstroke, and sidestroke; swim underwater; hold and carry swimmers; do the dead man's float for a half hour; and tread water fully clothed for ten to twenty minutes.

Even if you don't intend to work on the waterfront, it's still a good idea to get certified. Many camps want other staff members to know first aid and CPR as well, and having that knowledge gives camp directors extra flexibility because others can fill in on aquatic duties if a staff is shorthanded. Some camps offer these classes as a seminar for staffers at the beginning of the summer.

Working at a camp looks great on a resume. The job instills more responsibility than running a drive-through or cooking fries, but do your homework to find out how much you'll earn. Some camps take counselors on a volunteer basis. As a high school student living at home, the experience alone might be worth it. But if you're a college student and need to sock away some money over the summer for school, you'll probably need to keep the pay in mind.

Fire and Rescue

Firefighting isn't the only task assigned to fire departments. Because most fire departments combine fire service with rescue service, calls come in that can involve anything from containing dangerous chemical spills to performing underwater rescues after traffic accidents. Underwater rescue teams are trained to dive in oceans, lakes, and dark canals. They know how to operate with zero visibility, feeling their way along the bottom with their hands, searching for a submerged car or body.

Because firefighters have to be prepared to handle any type of call, most firefighters are cross trained. Cross training helps fire departments get as much of the crew involved in an emergency as needed. For example, firefighters can extricate victims trapped in a car wreck or perform high-angle rescues, rappelling off the tops of buildings.

Every emergency requires specific skills. Firefighters don't want to arrive at a scene and discover there's no one there to handle a certain problem. Cross training is also more cost-effective for the fire department and the taxpayers and is certainly more interesting for all of the firefighters.

Getting Started

Competition for firefighting jobs gets more competitive all the time. Although the work can be demanding and contains an element of significant risk, the jobs are also stable—laying off firefighters is never popular for city governments—and provide good pay and benefits. Most fire departments expect you to have undergone training before you even apply for a job. If you're serious about working as a firefighter, the best way is to get some training first. You can take a twelve-week firefighter training program or study in a two-year program for an associate's degree in fire science.

Once hired, firefighters continue their training, either on their own or through in-house classes. All skills must be kept current, and there are also many specialties to learn.

It is also wise to have good verbal and written skills. Firefighters are often called on to speak in front of groups, and they must know how to write reports. Math and chemistry are important, too, and those who want to climb the administrative ladder should take business and management courses.

But academics are only one part of it. Firefighters must also have physical and emotional strength. They wear heavy gear and carry heavy equipment—and regularly run across upsetting situations. Being able to cope is a necessity.

To further enhance your employability, it's a good idea to get some related experience first. Volunteer fire departments still make up a large percentage of our country's firefighting force. They usually accept trainees who are still in school.

To get an idea of what firefighting exams are like and what skills are involved, check out one or more of the following books:

Firefighter Exams, by James J. Murtagh (Barron's), 2006
Firefighter's Handbook: Essentials of Firefighting and Emergency Response (Thomson Delmar Learning), 2004
Master the Firefighter Exam, by Fred M. Rafilson (Arco), 2005

These will help you understand what kind of knowledge you need to have going into your firefighting exam. *The Firefighter's Handbook* is a common text used in many firefighting courses.

Specializing

Once on the force, you have a number of options open to you. To get on a specialist team—underwater rescue, hazardous materials, and so forth—you first have to exhibit a desire to do the work. Then there has to be an opening on a particular team. But even more important, the team has to feel you would make a good addition. Members have to trust you and have confidence in your ability to learn.

Underwater Rescue. Each team requires certain training or skills. For example, underwater rescue experts are trained as certified divers. They have to be expert swimmers first, with strength and endurance. In addition to the skills every scuba diver learns, underwater rescue divers must know how to work in pitch-black conditions, in freezing water, or in dangerous rapids or unpredictable tides. They must also be familiar with the equipment of the trade, such as grappling hooks and inflatable boats.

Specialist firefighters are a part of the regular combat firefighting team. An underwater rescue specialist, for example, does not respond only when there's a call about a submerged car with passengers. He or she is prepared, just as every firefighter is, to answer any sort of emergency call that comes into the station.

EMTs. Because fire departments provide so many services in addition to firefighting, most require members of their forces to be emergency medical technicians (EMTs) or paramedics. EMTs are versed in the basics of first aid and lifesaving. They learn CPR, patient handling, extrication, and the basics of medical illnesses and injuries. Essentially, EMTs provide basic life support. They're expected to arrive on the scene and take care of a patient until the paramedics get there. If the EMTs and paramedics arrive together, then the EMTs assist the paramedic.

If the EMT is working in an area of the country where higher-level paramedics are not a part of the team, he or she is then responsible for getting the patient to the hospital. An EMT might also be responsible for driving the ambulance. In addition to fire-fighting EMTs, EMTs also work for private ambulance companies and in emergency rooms in some hospitals.

Paramedics. Paramedics have to be EMTs before becoming paramedics. They are trained in very sophisticated, advanced levels of life support. Their goal is to keep a patient alive, and they function in the field as an extension of the physician. They are the prehospital hands, eyes, and ears of the doctor and must be able to assess a situation and react the way a doctor would.

When possible, paramedics contact the hospital and let the doctor know what they've done for the patient. Some ambulances or rescue trucks are capable of transmitting medical data such as electrocardiograms (EKGs) by radio to the hospital. At this point, the doctor can let the paramedics know if there is anything else that should be done before bringing in the patient. Paramedics have a strong relationship with physicians, who have learned over time to trust the paramedics' training and expertise.

In addition to fire departments, paramedics also work with city or county agencies, for hospitals, and for private ambulance companies.

Emergency Training. EMTs can generally be trained in six to twelve weeks through a community college. During the course of the program, they spend time observing in hospitals and gaining practical experience riding in ambulances.

To become certified, EMTs are given a practical exam through the school and a written exam through the state or province. (For links to certifying agencies, check the National Registry of

Emergency Medical Technicians website at www.nremt.org/ EMTServices/emt_cand_state_offices.asp or the Paramedic Association of Canada's website at www.paramedic.ca.) Once you have become a certified EMT, you can then go on to paramedic school. Most programs are offered through community colleges, and that is the most popular route, though there are a few private paramedic training schools. The training for a paramedic could take anywhere from two or three semesters to two years, depending upon the state or province in which you live.

The course of study for a paramedic is a full curriculum with course work that includes anatomy, physiology, pharmacology, the administration and interpretation of EKGs, medical diagnoses, handling cardiac arrests, defibrillation, and related medical subjects.

Paramedic trainees spend a lot of time in hospitals learning advanced techniques. They work in operating rooms with anesthesiologists learning intubation, the process of inserting a tube into a patient's windpipe. They also spend time on hospital critical care floors, learning from the nurses how to take care of patients. In addition, trainees also participate in births and learn about pediatrics.

Both firefighting EMTs and paramedics learn about the different lifesaving equipment available to them, including extrication devices, air splints, pediatric immobilizers, suction units, and portable defibrillating and EKG machines.

Fire and Rescue Salaries

Firefighters earned a median hourly wage of $18.43 in 2004, which corresponds to $37,000 annually, without consideration for overtime. First-line supervisors of firefighters earned an average of $59,000 annually.

EMTs and paramedics earned an average of just over $25,000 in 2004, though top earners can bring in salaries in the mid-forties and higher in the most expensive North American cities. Earning potential rises substantially over the years as experience increases, and the demand for both EMTs and paramedics should expand rapidly through the mid-2010s as baby boomers age and cities phase out volunteer programs in favor of professionals.

What It's Really Like

Few people can truthfully say that what they do is a matter of life and death, but paramedics and EMTs save lives all the time, and the sense of purpose they draw from their calling has nothing to do with dollars.

Lieutenant Woodrow "Woody" Poitier, Paramedic/Firefighter

Woody Poitier actually became a paramedic before he became a firefighter. He was in the first group of twelve—affectionately called the Dirty Dozen—that his city in South Florida hired when its paramedic program was started in 1975. As a veteran of emergency medicine, he has seen and done just about everything, and he takes his job seriously and also gets a lot of satisfaction out of making a crucial difference in others' lives.

"My main duty is to preserve life and limb," Poitier explains. He's now a paramedic supervisor, so he doesn't go out on every call, but he does usually jump in for those that involve trauma or children.

Trauma Mysteries and Philosophy. Poitier has seen shootings, stabbings, cuttings, and drownings. "You get the drunk drivers who cause so many accidents, but most of the time they don't even get hurt," he says. "The Lord takes care of children, fools, and drunks." Children, he says, are the most resilient. Even if they get hurt, they seem to have the ability to jump right back.

Even so, paramedics can't accurately predict who will make it and who won't. "I've seen calls where everything has gone right, we have dynamite paramedics on the scene, yet you can't save the victim," he says. "Then other times, everything seems to go wrong;

you can't get an IV started, nothing seems to be working, and yet he lives. There's no rhyme or reason. I do know the paramedics do a good job."

Poitier estimates that he's delivered fourteen babies, most of them in the back of ambulances on the interstate. One lady named her child after him. "Even if you are able to help only one person in a twenty-four-hour period, it makes it worth it," he says.

Nuisance Work. Paramedics also have to stock the truck and make sure all the equipment is functioning and accurate. They write reports on the patients they see as well. As you can imagine, with life hanging in the balance, the steps a paramedic takes and the vitals of the patient going into the ER are of the utmost concern. "We also have controlled drugs on the trucks such as Valium and morphine, and we have to be very careful about that," Poitier says.

Not every call the paramedics get is an emergency. Some people feel that if they summon an ambulance, they'll get priority when they arrive in the emergency room. But if a person makes a complaint, EMTs and paramedics are obligated to take it seriously and transport him or her to the hospital, whether it's for a stubbed toe or a toothache that a guy has had for three days, and who decides to call at three o'clock in the morning because he can't fall asleep. "There's a lot of misuse of the system," Poitier says.

Advice from Woody Poitier. If you want a rewarding job and one that actually helps people, then this is the job to go into, Poitier says. "If you have an interest in medicine but don't want to go to great lengths to become a doctor, the paramedic field would be the way to do it."

Stress and high-pressure situations are inherent in the job. Expect to encounter people in severe distress, people who are depending on you to make the right choices and sustain them until they can get to a fully equipped facility. Sometimes people don't make it, and Poitier describes those times as the most difficult to handle, particularly when they're children. If you're sensitive to graphic imagery or get nauseated easily, this is the wrong job for you.

If you find that it's right, however, you won't have to question whether what you do is important. "After all these years I'm still gung ho," Poitier says. "Even when I'm off duty and I'm at home and hear the sirens go by, it gets the adrenalin going.

"Every emergency is different, and, believe it or not, you come into people's homes, their lives, and the positive energy you input always seems to have a positive result, and that's really, really rewarding."

National Park Service and Parks Canada

The National Park Service (NPS) employs more than twenty thousand permanent and temporary workers and 125,000 volunteers. Its mission is to manage and protect almost four hundred natural, cultural, and recreational areas in the United States, Guam, Puerto Rico, and the Virgin Islands. Its headquarters is in Washington, D.C., with seven regional offices, an interpretive design center, and a service center. Competition for jobs, especially at the most well-known sites, can be fierce. But the NPS employs a huge permanent staff, and this is supplemented tenfold by an essential seasonal workforce during peak visitation periods.

The best way for a newcomer to break in is to start off with seasonal employment during school breaks. With a couple of summer seasons under your belt, you should enhance your qualifications enough to compete well for permanent employment, although eventual full-time jobs are never guaranteed to seasonal staff. Office of Personnel Management regulations give some preference to veterans of the U.S. armed forces.

Internships are available, and interns are hired by individual parks, so you should determine where you want to work and apply directly. The Student Conservation Association (www.thesca.org) administers three volunteer and internship programs with stints ranging from three weeks to a year. Resource assistants work for the NPS and other federal agencies. If you're interested in a career or a seasonal job with the NPS, you can search job openings and apply online through the Office of Personnel Management (www.usajobs.opm.gov). Recruitment for summer employment runs September 1 to January 15. Some sites, such as Death Valley or Everglades National Park, also have a busy winter season. The winter recruitment period is June 1 to July 15.

Parks Canada (www.pc.gc.ca) manages more than forty national parks, including some of the wildest and most pristine territory in the world. Duties with Parks Canada are much the same as with the NPS. The agency employs four thousand (seven thousand during the summer), more than four hundred of which are park wardens, the equivalent to a ranger in the United States. The parks also hire cultural interpreters, archaeologists, tradespeople, and historians. Search for openings and apply online at Job Bank (www.jobbank.gc.ca).

Park Rangers and Wardens

The National Park Service hires three categories of park rangers (generally on a seasonal basis): enforcement, general, and interpretation. Duties vary greatly from position to position and site to site, but rangers in the general division are usually responsible for forestry or resource management; developing and presenting programs that explain a park's historic, cultural, or archeological features; campground maintenance; firefighting; lifeguarding; law enforcement; and performing search-and-rescue activities.

Rangers also sit at information desks, provide visitor services, or participate in conservation or restoration projects. Entry-level employees might also collect fees, provide first aid, and operate audiovisual equipment.

Wardens for Parks Canada also have a multidisciplinary roster of duties, from protecting and managing park resources to administering public safety programs, patrolling park roads, campsites, and backcountry and working with park neighbors to preserve surrounding ecosystems and address residents' concerns. On many levels, they are the first line of defense in attacks on the parks' integrity, in whatever form, and are perhaps their best advocates.

Education and Earnings

Park rangers should have at least two years of college with a minimum of twelve credits in science and criminal justice. Courses in natural resource management, natural or earth sciences, park and recreation management, archaeology, and anthropology are very helpful. Rangers also receive on-the-job training that is often supplemented with more formal training sessions. Six-month training programs are available at the Grand Canyon National Park in Arizona and at Harpers Ferry, West Virginia. The possibility for promotion would be to district ranger, park manager, or staff specialist. Further education may be required for these promotions.

Jobs with the service are competitive, and park budgets appear tighter than ever. Political tides might well determine the future market for park service personnel. Summer rangers with a college degree start at just under $19,000 annualized. Full-time rangers with degrees start between $21,000 and $32,000. Park wardens in Canada might start at Can$25,000 for seasonal work and earn between Can$45,000 and $60,000 as full-time wardens.

What It's Really Like

Look beyond the Smokey the Bear hat and badge and find out from a real park ranger what it's like to be a water-rescue expert.

Randy Justice, National Park Ranger

Randy Justice works for the National Park Service, a division of the U.S. Department of the Interior, at Big South Fork National

River and Recreation Area in Tennessee and Kentucky. He earned his B.S. in recreation resource management at Northern Arizona University in Flagstaff. He has also participated in many training programs, such as law enforcement, swift-water rescue, and basic boating and seamanship courses offered by the U.S. Coast Guard.

Justice has worked at eight parks in his career, starting with Lake Powell, then Death Valley; Grand Canyon; Washington, D.C.; Shenandoah; Lowell National Historical Park (near Boston); Valley Forge; and Big South Fork National River and Recreation Area.

Formative Years. Justice has spent most of his life in the backcountry. In his teens, he started paying attention to news reports of people who had gotten into trouble in the backcountry. He also started seeing the damage inflicted on the environment by careless people. "I wanted to be involved, doing something about this," Justice says.

He began getting search-and-rescue training in college, when he joined the Coconino County (Arizona) Search and Rescue team and learned high-mountain rescue and rappelling techniques. His first taste of water rescue came at the National Park Service Ranger Academy at California's Santa Rosa Community College. "We spent several days on the Russian River," he says. "The water was forty-three degrees, and we were in [level]-four rapids." Level-six rapids are considered unrunnable. The Swiftwater Rescue Training course covered approaching and stabilizing a victim in moving water, use of throw bags and rescue boards, swimming in rapids, building and operating a tyrolean, use of the tripod method for crossing moving water, and rope work and knots associated with swift-water rescue. Justice has since been recertified.

While in college he met a ranger for the first time, the father of a college roommate and a twenty-year veteran of the National Park Service. Justice started going to the Grand Canyon to visit with them and was soon hooked. After college he got a job with the NPS as a seasonal ranger at Lake Powell, on the Arizona-Utah border, focusing on recovery of bodies. The lake is two hundred miles long and has two thousand miles of coastline. It's also six hundred feet deep. "Some of its victims are still there," he says.

Eventually he took a job as a federal police officer with the Department of Defense at Walter Reed Army Hospital in Washington, D.C., which granted him career-conditional status so that he would be able to compete for permanent government jobs. Once in the National Park Service system, you can compete for positions as they become available, though the competition is very intense.

On the Job. "Boring is not in a ranger's vocabulary," Justice says. His day might start at three in the morning with a call from the dispatcher sending him to look for a lost child, go to a car accident, or participate in the rescue of rafters stranded in the river during an unexpected flood. The National Park Service is considered one of the most highly trained agencies in the government, but expertise depends on the park. Some of the parks have a lot of law enforcement, and some focus on resource management. Lowell and Big South Fork have had the most water rescues and recoveries.

Even at Big South Fork, water rescues are just a small part of his job. Most of his job is resource based: a lot of patrolling, including running the white water in rafts and kayaks. He is also a federal police officer, an EMT, a wildland firefighter, a helicopter crew member, a self-defense instructor, and a DARE officer. "Sixteen-hour days are not unusual" during the busy season, Justice says. "A forty-hour workweek is a rarity, and there are no time clocks." Sometimes he goes on special details anywhere in the country that can last for twenty-one days. For example, he has provided security for two presidents, a vice president, and several dignitaries.

Struggling to Make a Difference. Justice laments that he sees people making the same mistakes that they did decades ago when he started. "Even with all the education and communication, I still see people ill prepared, drinking and driving or boating, and young men suffering from machismo," he says. Lowell's five miles of historical canals near Boston were a magnet for the neighborhood kids. In Justice's two and a half years there, he helped recover seven bodies; six were preteens.

Yet in his outreach to the community, he can see the difference he's making on a regular basis. "One day I was on patrol in a marked car when I came upon a serious bike accident," he says. "One of the bystanders saw me and said, 'There's someone who can help.' That means something to me." He's been on bike patrol before and ended up with a dozen kids following him on bikes pretending they're rangers. And as a DARE officer, he provides instruction about water safety to children and adolescents.

Those interactions give him the kind of reward he can't find in a paycheck. "No one does this for the money," he says. Justice says most permanent rangers are either GS-7 or GS-9 employees: an entry-level GS-7 made $32,000 in 2007, and a top-tier GS-9 could earn $51,000, not counting overtime pay.

Advice from Randy Justice. Aspiring rangers and wardens should be mindful that the work itself must be its own reward. We have already covered the pay scale. Similarly, rangers and wardens don't often get to bask in the role of hero. "Many of the people they rescue or assist won't even acknowledge the work that the rangers have done," Justice says. "They take it for granted that someone will be there to assist them when they get themselves in trouble." Another downside for water rescues is that most of the time they are recovering bodies. Rangers usually aren't able to respond fast enough to save someone in the few minutes that it takes to drown.

Look for training from the Coast Guard Auxiliary, adult education services, and local colleges. If there's a rescue team in your community, ask to speak with them and see firsthand what is involved. Physical stamina is important, and many rescue calls will come when you least expect them. "Remember that keeping yourself safe is as important as helping others," Justice says. "This year I was recertified in swift-water training from the same agency that I was first trained by. . . . It was tougher this time around!"

CHAPTER SEVEN

Teaching and Guiding in Aquatic Sports

That old adage, "those who can, do; those who can't, teach," couldn't be further from the truth when it comes to aquatic sports. To teach swimming, diving, boating, windsurfing, and all the other water sports, instructors first must be proficient in the necessary skill area—and in many cases certified by a particular organization, such as the Red Cross or PADI, the Professional Association of Diving Instructors.

In Chapter 6, we learned about all the possible places for water safety and rescue. Those same settings afford recreation, too. Those with the right aquatic skills can become instructors in their areas of expertise. Aquatic sports include:

Canoeing
Charter boating
Charter fishing
Kayaking
Motorboating
Sailing
Scuba diving
Snorkeling
Swimming
Waterskiing
Windsurfing

Aquatic-related instruction centers around the usual adult spheres of recreation but also includes a few you might not have thought of.

- **Civic pool facilities and community centers.** City pools and community centers usually offer summer and year-round programs in swim instruction and other aquatic sports. Even if the facility hasn't posted openings online or in its newsletter, you can still inquire about openings or submit a resume. They might keep it on file for reference when something opens up.
- **College campuses.** Many colleges and universities offer physical education majors and need qualified instructors for their various programs. In most cases you need an advanced degree in physical education or a related field to land a job in a university setting.
- **Condos and residential developments.** Some condos and planned communities that emphasize lifestyle hire life-guards or swim instructors to provide classes to children and adult residents. Look for openings online, or keep an eye out for new developments with pools in fast-growing parts of town.
- **Continuing education programs.** Most adult and continuing education programs offer aquatic sports instruction, from basic swimming to sailing and diving, and hire experienced instructors to carry out their programs. Consult your local board of education, library, or community college, or check the phone book under adult or continuing education.
- **Dive shops.** For certified dive instructors, the first place to start your job search would be through local dive shops. They often sponsor dive training and would also know of other organizations in the area offering the same thing.

- **Gyms.** Many gyms and athletic clubs offer swim instruction. They also provide coaching for professional athletes or swimmers in training for competition. The YMCA/YWCA is one of the biggest employers of youth leaders, recreation workers, activity and specialty instructors, and related positions. Jobs are filled both in YMCA and YWCA city and town centers as well as at a variety of Y-sponsored resident and day camps around the country. Contact your local Y for information on job openings and requirements.
- **Hospitality industries.** Country clubs, hotels, and resorts often have pools or lakeside or beachfront property. They may operate boating, diving, and windsurfing schools. Search websites and phone book listings to find out what sort of amenities they have, or make the rounds in person.
- **Marinas and yacht clubs.** Yacht clubs are obvious places to look for jobs teaching sailing and other types of boating.
- **Summer camps.** Day and resident summer camps are one of the largest employers of aquatic sports instructors. Typically camps offer swimming, canoeing, and sailing, and some camps specialize in a particular activity, such as windsurfing or diving.

The best advice camping professionals will give you is to start early to find that job. Many jobs are lined up as much as a year in advance, taken by counselors and other staff members who plan to work every summer for a particular camp.

In the Appendix, you will find a list of national organizations offering camping programs. When you make contact with them, be specific about the employment information you are seeking and the geographic location in which you would like to work. Some of these organizations accept resumes and will forward them to local councils.

Getting Started

Some employers do not require specific certifications for some positions. For others, if you can demonstrate that you are a competent windsurfer, for example, and have the skills all instructors require—patience and the ability to teach—you might find the job is yours. Sports such as swimming or diving, however, require extensive training and certification before you can teach. Here are a couple of examples:

Swim Instructors

Swim instructors are probably the most plentiful of recreational aquatic jobs. Because swimming is such an important skill to have, more people take lessons for swimming than for any other water-oriented activity. Instructors should have certifications in adult, child, and infant CPR and first aid training through the Red Cross. The gold standard for swim instructor certification is the Red Cross's Water Safety Instructor (WSI). Many operations require it. The program is as follows:

RED CROSS WATER SAFETY INSTRUCTOR CERTIFICATE

- **Purpose:** Train instructor candidates to teach the Red Cross Swimming and Water Safety Program. Students learn how to run training sessions and how to evaluate participants' progress.
- **Certification requirements:** Successfully participate in course activities, meet instructor candidate competencies, and pass a written test with a minimum score of 80 percent.
- **Prerequisites:** Must be at least sixteen years old. Must possess an Instructor Candidate Training certificate issued in the last twelve months or a current Health and Safety Services instructor authorization and successfully complete the precourse session consisting of tests of water safety and swimming skills and knowledge.

- **Course length:** Approximately thirty hours (including the precourse session).
- **Certification validity:** Authorization is for two years.

Swim instructors commonly come up from the ranks of lifeguards and may be able to earn extra money by serving as a lifeguard or head lifeguard when not instructing. Pay is somewhat higher for instructors than for lifeguards, usually by about $2 per hour. Hourly wages run about $10 to $12, depending on location and experience.

Instructors working for a private club or offering private lessons may make considerably more, particularly if they aren't employed by a community organization.

For information on swim instructors, lifesaving, and lifeguard courses, contact your local Red Cross (www.redcross.org; www.redcross.ca) or YMCA/YWCA (www.ymca.net, www.ywca.org, www.ymca.ca, and www.ywcacanada.ca).

Diving Instructors

There are four or five nationally and internationally recognized certifying agencies for dive instructors, such as PADI, the Professional Association of Diving Instructors (www.padi.com), and NAUI Worldwide, the National Association of Underwater Instructors (www.naui.com). Certified courses in basic diving and then instructor training are offered through colleges and universities, the YMCA and YWCA, adult education, and dive shops.

Each certifying body has its own requirements for recognizing the accomplishments of dive instructors. Most require a step progression, from diver to assistant instructor to dive master to full instructor.

NAUI Instructor Levels. There are several instructor levels offered by NAUI. Here are just two: assistant instructor (AI) and dive master.

- **Assistant instructor.** As an assistant instructor, you would be authorized to teach all aspects of skin and scuba diving under the supervision of a NAUI instructor. This is the best possible way to develop your instructional skills. The rating can be a step toward full instructor or an end in itself. The program is designed to introduce students to diving instruction basics. It also tests individuals in fundamental water skills needed to be capable assistants. You can obtain additional training or experience if you wish to assist in highly specialized training activities, such as deep-sea, wreck penetration, cavern, or ice dives.

- **Dive master.** An active-status NAUI dive master, one step below full instructor, is qualified to organize and conduct dives for certified divers if the diving activities and locales approximate those in which the dive master is trained. Additional training, knowledge, or experience is necessary for the dive master who desires to organize highly specialized activities, such as wreck penetration, cavern, or ice dives, or to enter a new locale. An active-status NAUI dive master is qualified to assist an active-status NAUI instructor in diving courses. If all other prerequisites are met, a current NAUI dive master is qualified to enter a NAUI Instructor Training Course (ITC). (Attending a NAUI Instructor Preparatory Program and NAUI Assistant Instructor certification are recommended prior to attending an ITC.)

Most instruction jobs are for the basic-level scuba enthusiast, so many dives are elementary in nature, and dive instructors often are expected to pitch in where other help is needed, such as hauling gear, captaining boats, or filling in at the dive shop. Because jobs usually are related to tourism, they are often located in beautiful coastal areas that many would envy. That perk is somewhat offset by the pay, which tends to be paltry. The cost of living in tourist towns is high, and salaries for dive instructors average

$15,000 to $20,000 per year, although that does not include tips, which could add 50 percent or more to an instructor's income. Instructors might be paid per dive, per day, or per month, so precise salaries may hinge on seasonality and how much an instructor works. Some resorts provide housing for instructors, and they may be able to earn more with additional certifications, moonlighting with extra classes, or working other dive-related jobs. Dive instructors are expected to provide their own equipment.

Charter Skipper

Not all water sports jobs involve teaching. Charter skippers take passengers out to sea, usually for fishing or diving expeditions but sometimes for snorkeling or sightseeing. The skipper acts as fishing expert, deckhand, and host. Much of a charter skipper's role is that of an ambassador, and he or she must be cordial and able to relate to many different personalities. If the boat is large enough, say forty feet or more, the captain might have a helper to work the boat and serve meals and drinks.

A fishing charter boat captain typically owns his or her own boat, and that is the captain's principal livelihood. Many charter skippers often work as staff for charter companies or as freelance charter skippers, much like instructors. And, in most cases, they, too, have a helper who works with them, taking care of the boat and serving meals and drinks. Charter skippers can operate at local levels, taking people fishing or just out for a day on the water, then back to the marina, or they can operate for days at a time, weeks sometimes, aboard a large vessel moving from one locale to another.

Qualifications. The first step any hopeful charter skipper must take is a bit of self-appraisal. Before candidates can take their certification exam, they must demonstrate that they have had a substantial amount of experience, usually years. Regulations for commercial sailors are administered by the U.S. Coast Guard

(www.uscg.mil/stcw) and by Transport Canada (www.tc.gc
.ca/marinesafety/mpsp/menu.htm). Start by reviewing their regulations and test standards.

Candidates may have to travel to another city and should plan
on staying all day for taking the test. Tests cover a wide variety of
marine topics, including inland and international rules of the
road, navigation, fire science, sound and light signals, and relevant
federal regulations. The questions often have little to do with pleasure boating and more to do with formal merchant marine rules
and regulations, boat handling, and seamanship. A license is a
necessary step in any professional captain's career and will open
many doors that might be otherwise remain closed.

Other Skills. Many good charter skippers bring a variety of skills
to their trades. They might speak another language, play a musical instrument, or be a great storyteller. Many crew members have
been trained in a variety of cooking skills and preparing drinks.
The skipper must be an expert at keeping the boat and all its systems in proper working order. A charter skipper must also know
the waters, the cruising grounds he or she will be operating in, and
often the little-known anchorages or stop-offs that offer some
unique attraction. Knowledge of the area's history also helps.
Charter guests often have a million questions about where they
are, so good skippers should have answers.

No matter how skilled a charter skipper may be in seamanship,
boat handling, navigation, and other related skills, they are
remembered by guests for the ambience they provide, by making
others feel at home and secure.

Earnings. Salaries for charter boat captains are all over the map
and depend on whether the captain also owns the boat, the size of
the boat, the market for charter cruises in a given location (is it a
hot honeymoon spot or known for its incredible fishing?), and
seasonality and how frequently the captain works. A common
baseline rate for skippers is $100 per person per day for a boat

under one hundred feet, but that may not include meals, drinks, or additional amenities, such as equipment rental, and a 10 percent tip is customary. A savvy businessperson in an ideal location could do quite well, making well over six figures; others earn enough to get by. Independent skippers bear the extra expense of marketing and promotion, insurance, boat payments, and maintenance.

What It's Really Like

Guide and instructor positions can be transitional summer jobs or lifelong careers. Swimming instructor Claire est and sailing instructor Lee Woods represent the range of possibilities.

Claire Best, Swimming Instructor

Claire Best has worked as a swim instructor both at a resident Girl Scout camp and for a metropolitan YMCA in New England. Like so many who have found a niche during their youth on a camp staff, she began by attending as a camper herself for years, and she couldn't get enough. "Between the time I was eight and nineteen, I spent almost every summer of my life at a variety of camps, in one capacity or another," she says. She started with day camps, camped overnight by age twelve, and became a CIT, a counselor in training, at age seventeen.

Preparation. Best says her years as a camper paved the way for her work as a counselor. In many cases, she had already learned a lot of the skills she would later be teaching to campers. "Swimming was my strongest area, and by the time I was sixteen I had passed my Red Cross junior and then senior lifesaver tests," she says. She got her first paying camp job as a swim and canoeing instructor at a Girl Scout camp in Maine. Two years later, she was a general counselor at another camp. In college she did similar work in a work-study program, employed by the local YMCA as a swim instructor and youth counselor.

On the Job. At Best's camp, swim instructors spent all day on the waterfront. They hung out on the dock or in the water teaching beginner, intermediate, and advanced swimmers. "With the little children, you had to be in the water with them, both for their safety and to reassure them as well as to demonstrate," Best says. "The older children who were better swimmers needed less demonstration, so, if you didn't feel like getting wet on a certain day, you could just set them to swimming laps. I'd call out instructions to help them improve their strokes." Her voice would be hoarse by the end of the day, and she confesses to having felt "waterlogged" sometimes. "But it was a great way to spend the summers, in the sun all day."

Overall Best views it as a good opportunity and an ideal social setting, where the days are free and easy and don't feel much like work. She liked the commotion in the dining hall, living in a rustic cabin in a wooded setting, the campfires at night, the songs, the skits, and the sports competitions. "It was like a paid vacation," she says. "The salaries were pretty horrendous, but you got room and board and a couple of days off here or there to explore the surrounding area." And on top of everything, she made great friends.

Advice from Claire Best. Best did not earn her Red Cross Water Safety Instructor certification, and considers herself lucky to have found a job without it. The YMCA followed a different swimming program than the Red Cross at the time, so possessing WSI status wasn't as important. These days, however, the more certification you have, the better—and better-paying—it is for you.

Lee Woods, Sailing Instructor and Charter Skipper

Lee Woods works on staff at Diamond 99 Marina in Melbourne, Florida, an affiliate of the American Sailing Association and one of about one hundred affiliates in the United States, Caribbean,

Canada, and Europe. He is a sailing instructor and a charter skipper.

Woods earned his B.A. in journalism from the University of Miami in 1973 and pursued graduate studies in science communication at Boston School of Public Communications and at an MIT summer program in technical writing. He is also a certified instructor in basic sailing, coastal cruising, and coastal navigation and has a U.S. Coast Guard captain's license.

How It All Began. Woods struck a deal with a friend of his not long after they started college. He would teach his friend guitar if the friend would, in turn, teach him to sail. "From the moment I first saw a sailboat on the water, sails full, leaning slightly, cutting through the water, I was hooked," Woods says. "I had to learn."

Journalism was Woods's primary focus at the time, but earning a living sailing gradually took priority. This was an adventure he could undertake in his Florida hometown, an ideal location for sailing. In the beginning, however, it was something that he simply wanted to master. Learning the rudiments of sailing was frustrating, as any new and challenging learning experience is, but he kept practicing on his own, making mistakes and learning. As time allowed, he would tag along with friends and help crew their boats.

He signed up for courses at the Indian River Sailing Club in Indian Harbor Beach, Florida, and remained a part of that group for several years, earning student certifications in several levels of sailing. As he progressed, he had a desire to teach as well as learn, which brought him to the American Sailing Association's Instructor Certification Clinic in Punta Gorda, Florida, on the Gulf Coast, a rigorous program designed to test and certify instructors. He earned his instructor ratings there. Shortly thereafter—and after more than fifteen years of experience—he took the exam for his U.S. Coast Guard captain's license. The license must be renewed every five years and requires written proof of ongoing work in the marine industry, so like aviation, sailing must be a serious pursuit in order to stay current.

Transitioning to Teaching. Upon taking up instructing, Woods soon realized that there was much more to consider than just technical expertise. "Too many instructors feel that if they know how to sail, they know how to teach," Woods says. "Not so. A good instructor will put as much study into teaching techniques as he or she will into sailing skills." He wanted to set as good an example as possible and minimize hazards to students, so he studied diligently to become a near-flawless sailor.

Woods also reluctantly had to acknowledge that sailing schools are businesses, with profits and losses just like any other business. Owners must deal with insurance issues, personal and training-facility liabilities, and promotion. The training boat needed to be in top shape; the gear clean, functional, and safe; and a strategy in place to teach that day's lesson. Woods also had to play the taskmaster, reminding some students that they hadn't paid the full amount and would have to do so before he could begin the class. Inevitably, someone would be unable to make one of the scheduled sailing dates, and he would have to figure out how to have them make that up.

On the Job. The same blend of sailing and instructional challenges that Woods must consider in planning and preparation also affects his experience on the water. "There is a bit of apprehension, as an instructor, in that you don't want to make too many mistakes," he says, both for his credibility's sake and for the safety of the students. A good instructor, he says, will not take beginners out on a day of bad weather. Students have an inherent fear of the unknown and what they cannot control, and they won't learn anything if they are in emotional or physical distress. "If they are frightened enough, they may not return for the second lesson," Woods says.

Much of his work on the boat, then, is directed toward making students feel comfortable and establishing a friendly, productive environment in which to learn.

Students are all ages and temperaments, and they come from all walks of life. Potential personality conflicts, compounded by the unfamiliarity of the surroundings and confining nature of the boat, are to be avoided.

"An instructor must mix humor and relaxation," he says. "There is no room for Captain Bligh"—the infamous lieutenant of the HMS *Bounty*—"or anyone who yells at students." Woods philosophizes that instructors must examine their own temperaments and abilities to create a harmonious atmosphere where stupid questions do not exist and where everyone gets equal time learning the various methods and techniques.

Lessons. A typical first day for basic sailing involves meeting the students, letting them introduce themselves, and talking about the program and what it entails. Woods lets them know what to expect, tries to ease any fears they may have, and recommends necessary gear, such as gloves and boat shoes. After the social orientation, he introduces them to the boat and explains the parts and their purposes.

Once on the water, he has a primary goal of letting the students do the sailing and letting them make mistakes. An instructor follows a typical learning format: explain, demonstrate, let the students try, then reinforce through repetition—"and always compliment their achievements," Woods says.

Most basic sailing programs do not last more than twelve hours (three days, four hours each day), so a great deal of learning must take place quickly. "At the end of four hours, most students are overwhelmed, excited, thrilled, or scared to death!" he says. At the end of the day, Woods holds a review session, sometimes at a nearby restaurant or at the training facility, to reinforce the concepts learned that day, address concerns, and allow students to celebrate their successes. There he introduces sketches, photos, and other training aids to help students remember.

Advice from Lee Woods. Before you can think about teaching others, Woods says, you have to learn as much as you can about sailing yourself. Be a sponge. Learn to sail, and to sail well. Sign up for and take all the programs possible, then continue on to instructor ratings. Eventually, individuals interested in this line of work must take the U.S. Coast Guard captain's license exam. Any vessel used for anything other than pleasure must have a licensed captain aboard.

One mistake many hopefuls make is to try the route of learning from a friend or relative. "There are many excellent sailors who are not affiliated with an established program," Woods says, "but established programs do give students accepted, internationally acknowledged methods and techniques, something many lesser-prepared individuals cannot offer. Safety issues, for example, are often ignored when friends teach friends.

"You do not have to be an America's Cup skipper, but you must know the boat inside out and be prepared to handle any situation that might arise. Students will expect you to demonstrate skills and techniques competently. If you cannot, then you are not ready to become an instructor. As in any field, the instructor must know far, far more than he or she ever has to teach."

Woods recommends picking the brains of those who hang around marinas and people who will take you sailing with them. Many people make their way around the world volunteering as crew members. You can also get a feel for the world of sailing by picking up consumer magazines such as *Sail Magazine* (www.sailmag.com) and *Sailing World* (www.sailingworld.com).

With the proper technical knowledge and the right temperament and social presence, Woods says a charter skipper can captain a small fishing vessel on a lake or a corporate megayacht.

"Overall, the life of a sailing instructor or charter skipper is rich in reward, but only when all the homework has been done and only when instructors and skippers themselves continue to learn," Woods says.

"In all, if anyone loves to sail, loves to help people learn, the job of a sailing instructor is by far one of the most rewarding jobs anyone could have."

Resources and Professional Associations

Science Resources

American Cetacean Society
PO Box 1391
San Pedro, CA 90733
www.acsonline.org

American Fisheries Society
5410 Grosvenor Lane
Bethesda, MD 20814
www.fisheries.org

American Geophysical Union
2000 Florida Avenue NW
Washington, DC 20009
www.agu.org

American Society of Limnology and Oceanography
ASLO Business Office
5400 Bosque Boulevard, Suite 680
Waco, TX 76710
www.aslo.org

American Society of Mammalogists
PO Box 7060
Lawrence, KS 66044
www.mammalsociety.org

American Veterinary Medical Association
1931 North Meacham Road, Suite 100
Schaumburg, IL 60173
www.avma.org

Association of Zoos & Aquariums
8403 Colesville Road, Suite 710
Silver Spring, MD 20910
www.aza.org

Bedford Institute of Oceanography
PO Box 1006
Mail Station B501
Dartmouth, NS B2Y 4A2
Canada
www.bio.gc.ca

Environmental Careers Organization
30 Winter Street, Sixth Floor
Boston, MA 02108
www.eco.org

Geological Association of Canada
Department of Earth Sciences
Alexander Murray Building, Room ER4063
Memorial University of Newfoundland
St. John's, NL A1B 3X5
Canada
www.gac.ca

Gulf Coast Research Laboratory
University of Southern Mississippi
703 East Beach Drive
Ocean Springs, MS 39564
www.usm.edu/gcrl

International Association for Aquatic Animal Medicine
www.iaaam.org

International Marine Animal Trainers Association
www.imata.org

Marine Technology Society
5565 Sterrett Place, Suite 108
Columbia, MD 21044
www.mtsociety.org

National Marine Fisheries Service
1315 East-West Highway, Ninth Floor
Silver Spring, MD 20910
www.nmfs.noaa.gov

National Water Research Institute
Environment Canada
867 Lakeshore Road
PO Box 5050
Burlington, ON L7R 4A6
Canada
www.nwri.ca

Oceanography Society
PO Box 1931
Rockville, MD 20849
www.tos.org

The Society for Marine Mammalogy
PO Box 692042
Orlando, FL 32869
www.marinemammalogy.org

Student Conservation Association
689 River Road
PO Box 550
Charlestown, NH 03603
www.thesca.org

Women's Aquatic Network
PO Box 4993
Washington, DC 20008
www.womensaquatic.net

Military Resources

Air Force ROTC
551 East Maxwell Boulevard
Maxwell AFB, AL 36112
www.afrotc.com/colleges/detLocator.php

Army ROTC
www.goarmy.com/rotc/find_schools.jsp

Cadets Canada
National Defence Headquarters
Major-General Pearkes Building
101 Colonel By Drive
Ottawa, ON K1A 0K2
Canada
www.cadets.ca

Canadian Forces Recruiting
66 Slater Street
Ottawa, ON K1A 0K2
Canada
www.recruiting.forces.gc.ca

Directorate of Pay Policy and Development (Canadian
    military pay)
www.forces.gc.ca/dgcb/dppd/engraph/home_e.asp

Montgomery GI Bill (United States)
www.gibill.com

National Defence and Canadian Forces
National Defence Headquarters
Major-General George R. Pearkes Building
101 Colonel By Drive
Ottawa, ON K1A 0K2
Canada
www.forces.gc.ca

U.S. Navy/Marines ROTC
www.nrotc.navy.mil

U.S. Coast Guard
Coast Guard Headquarters
2100 Second Street SW
Washington, DC 20593
www.uscg.mil

U.S. military pay scales
www.dod.mil/militarypay/pay/bp/index.html

U.S. Marine Corps
www.usmc.mil

U.S. Navy
www.navy.mil

U.S. Navy Recruitment
www.navy.com

Commercial Fishing Resources

Additional information about fisheries can be obtained from the
following organizations.

National Fisheries Institute
7918 Jones Branch Drive, Suite 700
McLean, VA 22102
www.aboutseafood.com

National Fisherman
PO Box 7437
Portland, ME 04112
www.nationalfisherman.com

National Marine Fisheries Service (licensing)
1315 East West Highway, Ninth Floor
Silver Spring, MD 20910
www.nmfs.noaa.gov

U.S. Coast Guard Merchant Mariner Licensing &
  Documentation
Coast Guard Headquarters
2100 Second Street SW
Washington, DC 20593
www.uscg.mil/STCW

Merchant Marine Resources

Maritime school links can be found at:

www.hal-pc.org/~nugent/school.html

Additional information about merchant marine careers and certification can be obtained by contacting:

Transport Canada: Marine Personnel Standards and Pilotage
330 Sparks Street
Ottawa, ON K1A 0N5
Canada
www.tc.gc.ca/marinesafety/mpsp/menu.htm

U.S. Coast Guard Merchant Mariner Licensing &
   Documentation
Coast Guard Headquarters
2100 Second Street SW
Washington, DC 20593
www.uscg.mil/STCW

U.S. Department of Transportation Maritime Administration
Southeast Federal Center
1200 New Jersey Avenue SE
Washington, DC 20590
www.marad.dot.gov

Water Transportation Resources

Transport Canada: Marine Personnel Standards and Pilotage
330 Sparks Street
Ottawa, ON K1A 0N5
Canada
www.tc.gc.ca/marinesafety/mpsp/menu.htm

U.S. Coast Guard Merchant Mariner Licensing &
   Documentation
U.S. Coast Guard Headquarters
2100 Second Street SW
Washington, DC 20593
www.uscg.mil/STCW

U.S. Maritime Administration
400 Seventh Street SW
Washington, DC 20590
www.marad.dot.gov

U.S. Merchant Marine Academy
300 Steamboat Road
Kings Point, NY 11024
www.usmma.edu

Cruise Resources

American Canadian Caribbean Line
461 Water Street
PO Box 368
Warren, RI 02885
www.accl-smallships.com

Carnival Cruise Line
3655 Northwest Eighty-Seventh Avenue
Doral, FL 33178
www.carnival.com

Cruise Job Finder
www.cruisejobfinder.com

Cruise Line International Association
910 Southeast Seventeenth Street, Suite 400
Fort Lauderdale, FL 33316
www.cruising.org

Cruise Ship Jobs
www.cruiseshipjob.com

Cunard Line
24303 Town Center Drive, Suite 200
Valencia, CA 91355
www.cunard.com

Disney Cruise Line
PO Box 10238
Lake Buena Vista, FL 32830
www.disneycruise.disney.go.com

Florida-Caribbean Cruise Association
11200 Pines Boulevard, Suite 201
Pembroke Pines, FL 33026
www.f-cca.com

Holland America Cruise Line
300 Elliott Avenue West
Seattle, WA 98119
www.hollandamerica.com

Norwegian Cruise Line
7665 Corporate Center Drive
Miami, FL 33126
www.ncl.com

Porthole Cruise Magazine
4517 Northwest Thirty-First Avenue
Fort Lauderdale, FL 33309
www.porthole.com

Princess Cruises
24844 Avenue Rockefeller
Santa Clarita, CA 91355
www.princess.com

Royal Caribbean International
1050 Caribbean Way
Miami, FL 33132
www.royalcaribbean.com

Water Safety Resources

American Red Cross
National Headquarters
2025 E Street NW
Washington, DC 20006
www.redcross.org

Canadian Red Cross
National Office
170 Metcalfe Street, Suite 300
Ottawa, ON K2P 2P2
Canada
www.redcross.ca

International Association of Fire Fighters
1750 New York Avenue NW
Washington, DC 20006
www.iaff.org

National Association of Emergency Medical Technicians
PO Box 1400
Clinton, MS 39060
www.naemt.org

National Park Service
1849 C Street NW
Washington, DC 20240
www.nps.gov

National Registry of Emergency Medical Technicians
Rocco V. Morando Building
6610 Busch Boulevard
PO Box 29233
Columbus, OH 43229
www.nremt.org

Parks Canada
25 Eddy Street
Gatineau, QC K1A 0M5
Canada
www.pc.gc.ca

YMCA Canada
42 Charles Street East, Sixth Floor
Toronto, ON M4Y 1T4
Canada
www.ymca.ca

YMCA USA
101 North Wacker Drive
Chicago, IL 60606
www.ymca.net

YWCA Canada
75 Sherbourne Street, Suite 422
Toronto, ON M5A 2P9
Canada
www.ywcacanada.ca

YWCA USA
1015 Eighteenth Street NW, Suite 1100
Washington, DC 20036
www.ywca.org

Aquatic Sports Resources

American Alliance for Health, Physical Education, Recreation
& Dance
1900 Association Drive
Reston, VA 20191
www.aahperd.org

American Camp Association
5000 State Road 67 North
Martinsville, IN 46151
www.acacamps.org

American Sailing Association
5301 Beethoven Street, Suite 265
Los Angeles, CA 90066
www.asa.com

American Sportfishing Association
225 Reinekers Lane, Suite 420
Alexandria, VA 22314
www.asafishing.org

Boy Scouts of America
PO Box 152079
Irving, TX 75015
www.scouting.org

Boys and Girls Clubs of America
1275 Peachtree Street NE
Atlanta, GA 30309
www.bgca.org

Camp Fire USA
1100 Walnut Street, Suite 1900
Kansas City, MO 64106
www.campfire.org

Canadian Yachting Association
Portsmouth Olympic Harbour
53 Yonge Street
Kingston, ON K7M 6G4
Canada
www.sailing.ca

Cruising World
PO Box 420235
Palm Coast, FL 32142
www.cruisingworld.com

Commercial Diving Schools Directory
www.trade-schools.net/directory/diving-schools-directory.asp

Girl Guides of Canada
50 Merton Street
Toronto, ON M4S 1A3
Canada
www.girlguides.ca

Girl Scouts of USA
420 Fifth Avenue
New York, NY 10018
www.girlscouts.org

National Recreation and Park Association
22377 Belmont Ridge Road
Ashburn, VA 20148
www.nrpa.org

NAUI Worldwide (National Association of Underwater
    Instructors)
PO Box 89789
Tampa, FL 33689
www.naui.com

PADI (Professional Association of Diving Instructors)
30151 Tomas Street
Rancho Santa Margarita, CA 92688
www.padi.com

Sail Magazine
98 North Washington Street
Boston, MA 02114
www.sailmagazine.com

Sailing World
PO Box 420235
Palm Coast, FL 32142
www.sailingworld.com

Scouts Canada
1345 Baseline Road
Ottawa, ON K2C 0A7
Canada
www.scouts.ca

YMCA Canada
42 Charles Street East, Sixth Floor
Toronto, ON M4Y 1T4
Canada
www.ymca.ca

YMCA USA
101 North Wacker Drive
Chicago, IL 60606
www.ymca.net

YWCA Canada
75 Sherbourne Street, Suite 422
Toronto, ON M5A 2P9
Canada
www.ywcacanada.ca

YWCA USA
1015 Eighteenth Street NW, Suite 1100
Washington, DC 20036
www.ywca.org

About the Author

Blythe Camenson is a full-time writer with four dozen books and numerous articles to her credit. As director of Fiction Writer's Connection (FWC), a membership organization for new writers, she edits and writes for *Tidbits*, the FWC newsletter, provides a free critiquing service to members and free consultation and also teaches e-mail courses on writing query letters and synopses. In addition, she offers a mentoring program to help students get their novels started on the right track. Through these programs and FWC, she has helped answer the questions of hundreds of new writers.

Some of Blythe Camenson's books include *How to Sell, Then Write Your Nonfiction Book*; *Careers in Writing*; *Great Jobs for Communications Majors*; *Careers for History Buffs*; and many others, all published by McGraw-Hill. She is also the author of *Give 'Em What They Want: The Right Way to Pitch Your Novel to Agents and Editors* (Writer's Digest Books), coauthored with Marshall J. Cook.